Mastering
Credit Derivatives

market editions

Mastering
Credit Derivatives

A step-by-step guide to
credit derivatives and their application

ANDREW KASAPI

FINANCIAL TIMES

PRENTICE HALL

PEARSON EDUCATION LIMITED

Head Office:
Edinburgh Gate
Harlow CM20 2JE
Tel: +44 (0)1279 623623
Fax: +44 (0)1279 431059

London Office:
128 Long Acre, London WC2E 9AN
Tel: +44 (0)171 447 2000
Fax: +44 (0)171 240 5771

First published in Great Britain 1999

ISBN 0 273 63928 5

British Library Cataloguing in Publication Data
A CIP catalogue record for this book can be obtained from the British Library.

This publication is designed to provide accurate and authoritative
information in regard to the subject matter covered. It is sold with the
understanding that neither the author nor the Publishers is engaged in
rendering legal, investing, or any other professional service. If legal advice
or other expert assistance is required, the service of a competent
professional person should be sought.

The Publishers and contributors make no representation, express or implied,
with regard to the accuracy of the information contained in this book and
cannot accept any responsibility or liability for any errors or omissions that
it may contain.

10 9 8 7 6 5 4 3 2 1

Typeset by Northern Phototypesetting Co. Ltd, Bolton.
Printed and bound in Great Britain by Redwood Books, Trowbridge, Wiltshire

The Publishers' policy is to use paper manufactured from sustainable forests.

About the Author

Andrew J Kasapi is a specialist in the sale of credit derivatives and structured credit driven products. He has worked in SocGens relative value team FIMAT. Andrew currently works for Bridport Investor Services Ltd in London. The company is part of the Bridport group whose main office is in Geneva, Switzerland. Bridport is an independent fixed income and credit derivative agency broker. The Bridport credit derivatives team predominantly brings together credit default swap counterparties. Andrew has also worked as a credit risk consultant for IBM Trading & Risk Consultancy where he specialized in credit risk and market risk methodologies.

This book is dedicated to my wife Amber,
whose constant support has been an invaluable aid

CONTENTS

FOREWORD

Is anyone actually making any money in credit derivatives? Most of the dealers I speak to on a day-to-day basis say 'Absolutely'. Certainly performance must be a priority for many of those running Wall Streets' 15-odd credit derivative units.

So the credit derivative business is now a viable business, long past any preliminary investment stage. The growth in volume of transactions has been spectacular. Any one part of a financial institution that invests needs to have a thorough understanding as to the pros and cons of credit derivatives. Any one part of an academic institution wishing to understand the newest credit derivative products in the market will also find this book useful. Why are they used? Who uses them? What exactly is a credit derivative? What are the risks? What are the benefits? Most importantly: Should my institution or I get involved in using them? These are all reasonable questions that I try to answer. *Mastering Credit Derivatives* is written for someone who understands what a bond or a loan is and from this basic instrument knowledge I proceed to explain a relatively simple concept, buying protection and selling protection against default by a counterparty.

This book is designed to give readers a practical insight into credit derivative instruments, and what the latest uses and issues are. You will be introduced to basic concepts such as credit spreads, default and recovery amount. *Mastering Credit Derivatives* is designed from a user point of view, and tries to tackle the concept of credit derivatives via the mature capital markets route, instead of any theoretical academic approach. This is not rocket science: if you know what debt is, you are half way to understanding credit derivatives.

Russia's default on domestic and senior debt and Japan's banking crisis has created a great interest in credit default protection instruments. This is a topical subject because we have seen a European sovereign country default on its debt obligation, if it can happen to them …

This book's primary objective is to demystify complex credit derivative products, that up to now have been kept very much within select institutions of the international banking community (i.e. inter-bank). The real explosion of the use of credit derivatives will happen when small and middle tier banks, reinsurance, insurance and large corporate institutions familiarize themselves with these products. They can then approach their banks and brokers to help them put on these trades.

The default swap will one day be as common a product as a plain vanilla interest rate swap.

Most finance professionals know what an interest rate swap is, they should equally know what a credit default swap is.

INTRODUCTION

About this book

Essentially, I have divided this book into five areas:

- a general market overview on credit derivatives and the history of their emergence;
- the different kinds of credit derivative instruments (on and off balance sheet, pure and impure credit derivatives;
- the application of credit derivatives;
- regulatory issues associated with credit derivatives;
- the pricing of credit derivatives.

Each chapter or section will fall into one of these broad categories.

This book will focus on the credit default swap, total rate of return swap and credit linked note. Collaterized bond obligations are also covered in some depth. I try to focus on practical trading scenarios as much as possible and avoid any unrealistic or overly academic explanations and uses of credit derivatives. Wherever possible, I use real market data and trades to illustrate an application.

Introduction to credit derivatives and credit risk

What is credit risk?

It is important to begin any discussion of credit derivatives by looking at credit risk because the definition of credit risk provides the context within which credit derivatives need to be examined.

> **Credit risk** refers to the possibility that a borrower will fail to service or repay a debt on time.

Definition

The degree of risk is reflected in the borrower's credit rating, the premium it pays for funds – expressed in terms of a spread over some benchmark instrument or index – and the market price of its debt. As a matter of prudence, lenders often try to reduce their exposure to credit risk in various ways, e.g. refusing to make loans to weaker credits, requiring collateral and other credit enhancements, obtaining backup guarantees and insurance, diversifying their loan portfolio, and setting aside reserves to cover potential losses. But these defence mechanisms all have limitations and have been unable to prevent loan losses, especially during economic downturns.

Part of the problem is that credit risk actually encompasses two variables: market risk (the possibility that market prices or rates will move in an adverse direction); and firm-specific risk (the possibility that an individual borrower's circumstances may change for the worse). Until recently, lenders could easily protect themselves against the first type of risk, since every borrower's situation is unique. But credit derivatives now enable users to isolate, price and trade firm-specific credit risk by unbundling a debt instrument or basket of instruments into its component parts and transferring each risk to those best equipped to handle it.

What are credit derivatives?

Credit derivatives are among the most important financial innovations of the past several years. Credit derivatives address an ongoing void in the credit market: the need for standard contracts that facilitate credit risk transfer.

It is important to realize that credit exposure is one of the most difficult financial risks to hedge and replicate. 'Risky' bonds are hard to borrow, and credit sensitive financing markets are not always deep enough to facilitate efficient risk transfer. Likewise, in the cash market, desired credit exposures are constrained by the maturities, coupons, and availability of a given credit's marketable bonds or loans.

> **Key point**
>
> Credit derivatives increase the breadth of the credit market because they simultaneously deepen the market for hedging and investment.

Credit derivatives are tools that help credit managers, to act optimally. Though the genesis for credit derivatives was the commercial banks' need to manage loan concentrations and regulatory capital, the applications of these types of instruments are significantly more far-reaching (see Table I.1). These applications include hedging, arbitrage, tax management, and yield enhancement. Default swaps can also be used in balance sheet management. For example, a lower-rated institution can use a default swap to generate income off balance sheet by assuming the credit exposure of a higher-rated institution. In comparison, an outright loan to the same higher-rated credit would result in negative income.

Table I.1 Applications of default swaps by users

Investor	Buy protection	Sell protection
Domestic and foreign banks	Hedge, diversity, relationship management	Relative value, yield enhancement
Insurance companies	Hedge, diversity, tax management	Relative value, yield enhancement
Money managers	Hedge, diversity, tax management	Relative value
Securities dealers	Hedge, underwriting	Relative value
Corporations	Tax management, hedge	Reduce borrowing cost, yield enhance, leverage
Hedge funds	Arbitrage	Leverage

At present, the concept of credit risk transfer is new and evolving; the credit derivatives market has experienced dramatic growth since its inception approximately six years ago, but most of this growth has taken place only in the past year. At over $150 billion, the notional amount of swaps outstanding has more than tripled since the Office of the Comptroller of the Currency (OCC) began collecting data in early 1997 (see Table I.2).

Table I.2 Credit derivative positions of commercial banks

Q1/97	Q2/97	Q3/97	Q4/97	Q1/98	Q2/98
$15 billion	$30 billion	$45 billion	$60 billion	$100 billion	$130 billion

This data is a better gauge of growth than scale, because it includes neither contracts of nonbank financial intermediaries nor structured assets such as credit linked notes.

> In time, participants in the credit markets will need to have at least some familiarity with derivative counterparts, to the extent that cash assets and their derivatives are linked.

Key point

A generally held misconception about the most common credit derivative (default swap) is that their value is somehow more closely tied to a default event than to generic credit sensitive cash assets. In the following chapters, we look at credit derivative instruments, pricing, valuation and applications of credit default and total return swaps. Our approach is simpler than formalized treatments that apply credit portfolio concepts to modelling credit derivatives. Although these data intensive treatments of credit derivatives have laid the necessary groundwork for risk management regulatory guidance, they have also made credit derivatives appear overly complex.

Key point

In practice, default swap valuation is simple because both the underlying risk (credit) and contract structure (swap) are familiar to the marketplace.

Credit risk management

Any over the counter derivative product carries with it a credit risk exposure.

When looking at the issue of credit risk management, it is helpful to refer to the particularly interesting situation that exists in Asia. This is a classic emerging market, that highlights credit risk management issues. Credit risk management issues have a direct relevance to the use of credit derivatives, as will be explained later.

The volume of worldwide derivative trading has grown by phenomenal amounts in recent years. Dealers have to set aside enough capital to deal with:

- market movements
- default by counterparties.

Any over the counter derivative product carries with it a credit risk exposure. If the counterparty goes bust or refuses to pay, the dealer must replace or unwind the position at prevailing market rates. The dealer may not be able to unwind a commitment from a bankrupt counterparty, so the dealer has to compute how much they will lose in the event of default and the probability of default. These are all tasks that are quite tricky to perform particularly in the Asian market because there is a shortage of credit information and the liquid corporate bond market makes it difficult to compute the spreads.

There is little worldwide data on company defaults. Most borrowing has to be done by private loans rather than by publicly traded bonds. Rating agencies have been active only since the beginning of 1996. So there is not much historical data available. The lack of data means that dealers have to rely on guesswork rather than on models.

"You can throw science out of the window. There just isn't the universe of rated credit to use as a benchmark in estimating the probability of default."

A much higher proportion of the borrowers in Asia are of lower credit quality, so by definition, you have to be prepared to face more credit risks.

There are very loose disclosure requirements for Asian companies:

- transparency is the main problem for assessing credit risk, both for derivatives and for standard corporate lending;
- the biggest hurdle to doing business is disclosure;
- some of the publicly available information is, at best, opaque.

A dealer might have the publicly available information supplemented by a couple of due diligence meetings. This is still much less than is required by an agency for credit assessment. A certain commitment is required to find out information as well as the necessary appetite to handle credit risk. In my experience you cannot expect that the information will be just handed to you.

When defaults occur, in the US, average losses in the event of default are 30–35 per cent. In Singapore, the number rises to 40–50 per cent. In the Asia-Pacific region as a whole, it can be above 50 per cent.

The lack of highly developed financial laws and case histories dealing with defaults, creates even more problems in the Asia market. There isn't a history of rulings due to default. Dealers cannot be sure of their chances in court and they see the court as a last resort. The legal system is slow, and even if you win a case, it will take quite some time to gain access to the counterparty's assets. You may get a judgment in the US or UK but the only way to gain payment from a company may be to get the local courts to compel them to pay. Even so, the local court may not recognize the overseas decision, and even if it does, the process may be very slow.

Investors can overcome these obstacles, i.e. cross border legal risk, by making sure that the Asian counterparty has assets overseas that may be grabbed by the courts. If you win the case, they will be able to seize those assets.

Default models offer tremendous flexibility with a great deal of guesswork in the calibration. For example, a US-based model might require the input of corporate spreads. In Asia, these can only be guessed.

> The subjective element of credit analysis remains vitally important, especially in the developing world.

Since the derivatives markets are less liquid, you need to allow a longer holding period before you can unwind the trade – the 'close out' period. The longer it is, the more market risk you are taking since the market may move in the elapsed time. In developed countries, you assume a one week close out period. In developing countries, two or three weeks are the norm. The longer close out period contributes to a higher credit risk.

Some banks incorporate liquidity risk into their models by requiring a higher return on risk-adjusted capital. This is done rather than use a different method of calculating exposure.

On the other hand, many Asian financial institutions pose less of a credit risk than expected. In Asia the government may step in and save an institution rather than let it go bankrupt. So there is weight given to the prospect of government or regulatory support or intervention. The intrinsic creditworthiness of an Asian bank is probably higher than if the same bank was located in the US.

It is also very difficult in Asia to find staff who understand the statistical methods of dealing with credit risk. There is no shortage of traditional credit officers who make decisions based on a company's cash flow criteria. But people familiar with the highly quantitative approaches required for calculating the credit risk of a derivative counterparty are rare. Hong Kong headhunters say that derivative credit risk managers are able to earn much higher salaries in the Asia-Pacific region.

The question when dealing in Asia, is how all the above issues can be solved? The simplest option is to avoid one-way transactions with counterparties that have a poor or unacceptable credit risk profile. Citibank identifies the counterparties it wants to deal with and the products it wants to transact with them. The system includes a detailed, forward looking micro analysis of the business environment, where sectors and individual companies which are likely to be successful are identified.

CSFB rates every counterparty internally and individually. A deal has to fit within their book or it doesn't get done.

Collaterization

A counterparty will post a margin in cash with the dealer to cover costs in the event of a default. The practice is common in the US and Europe, but this method is not so popular in Asia. This approach is popular with dealers in general but not with companies who would rather use their cash elsewhere. Derivative dealers' salespeople and marketers have to convince the companies why collaterization is a required part of the deal.

> **Client education in credit enhancement is necessary.**

Key point

Collaterization does take up extra time and work, i.e. calculating margins, calling them, making sure they are posted, etc. Every counterparty would prefer to do without collaterization if it could.

Speculation

In Asia, some companies or individuals use derivatives to speculate. So, for example, a company may decide to enter a derivative transaction for no good business reason. The entrepreneur who owns the company may wish to speculate on the company's assets. However, it is important to try to avoid deals where shareholder voting is controlled by one rich individual and where the deal involves punting with the company's money. There is a long history of speculation driven disasters, where high margin exotic deals have turned into catastrophes. Some deals are turned down flat, for example a steel dealer who wants to punt in the forex market. An alternative is to convince the owner to do the deal through his personal account, using a collateral to back it up. This way, there is no possibility of the 'shareholders' voting to renege on the commitments.

Asia and credit derivatives

When dealing credit derivatives, there are occasions when you want to do the deal but are afraid of the counterparty risk.

For example, a dealer wants to do a deal with an attractive risk adjusted return on capital but the credit lines are all used up. Credit derivatives allow them to separate the deal from the credit risk. It means finding a third party willing to take on the credit risk, without taking on the market risk which is the *raison d'être* of the derivative structure.

> *When dealing credit derivatives, there are occasions when you want to do the deal but are afraid of the counterparty risk.*

Credit derivatives are gaining popularity in Asia. Local banks can leverage their knowledge of the individual companies and local credits and receive a premium for taking on the credit risk.

One popular type of deal is credit mediation. Say, for example, a US bank wants to deal with a Filipino company but does not have the required credit lines to do so. One solution would be to find a Filipino bank with a high credit rating, the US bank to do the deal with the Filipino bank, and the Filipino bank to do a mirror trade with the local Filipino company. In this way, the US bank only takes on the credit risk of the Filipino bank. The local bank has taken on the risk of the end user defaulting. The US bank has only taken on the risk of the Filipino bank defaulting. The Filipino bank incorporates a premium into the deal and so earns a spread between the deals to compensate it for the risk.

The above scenario is a familiar one. The US bank cannot be expected to be familiar with 100 counterparty names. Instead it just transacts with the three or four local banks which have local expertise.

An alternative way of structuring the deal would be for the US bank to deal directly with the counterparty and then do a credit default swap or a credit option with the local bank to remove the credit risk from the deal. This means that the local bank agrees to guarantee the obligations of the local end user in case of default or downgrade. Credit risks are difficult to deal with but, nonetheless, very important.

Understanding credit derivatives

Credit derivatives can be applied to satisfy the following credit risk management needs:

- management of credit lines
- regulatory capital offsets
- risk reduction and economic capital
- balance sheet benefits
- portfolio hedging.

The following risk managers are likely to use credit derivatives to satisfy these needs:

- *Banks.*
- *Insurance companies* – to manage commercial credit risk.
- *Corporates* – to isolate project finance credit risk.
- *Fund managers* – to hedge spread risk.

Market makers in credit derivatives must understand how to structure credit derivatives to meet risk managers' needs.

To do this we must understand the risk managers' objectives. An initial analysis of hedge availability and the optimal structure suitable for the given objectives are the first steps. An analysis of residual risks, such as basis and legal risks, is required. We must also adopt a pricing approach. Finally, we must understand how the regulator treats credit derivatives.

This book tries to address some of the key issues that are currently in debate amongst the major credit derivative participants. It is by no means written from an academic's viewpoint, but more from a user/ investor viewpoint.

The Emergence of the Credit Derivative Market

The potential of credit derivatives

How do we achieve the following objectives?

- We want to lend to Fiat but our country limit for Italy is full.
- We want to take exposure to Brazil without incurring US interest rate risk.
- We want six month exposure to the Philippines but there are no securities under two years in the market.

In 1993, investment bankers began to talk about a new class of structured products–credit derivatives. But, despite the talk, almost the only deals done were for the investment banks themselves. Clients weren't interested and hedging was next to impossible. But, at last, the talking is over and a significant number of transactions are now getting done.

The potential of credit derivatives is immense. There are hundreds of possible applications: for commercial banks which want to change the risk profile of their loan books; for investment banks managing huge bond and derivative portfolios; for manufacturing companies overexposed to a single customer; for equity investors in project finance deals with unacceptable sovereign risk; for institutional investors that have unusual risk appetites (or just want to speculate); even for employees worried about the safety of their deferred remunerations. The potential uses are so widespread that some market participants argue that credit derivatives could eventually outstrip all other derivative products in size and importance.

> *The potential of credit derivatives is immense.*

The first deals were done in 1993 when Bankers Trust and Credit-Suisse Financial Products (CSFP) in Japan began selling notes whose redemption value depended on specific default events.

"When the business started, it was about credit protection for the bank," says Philip Borg, a managing director at Bankers Trust at the time. *"We would sell a Bankers Trust note whose payout was linked to a credit event and a reference asset. We also did basket notes which referenced several names. The investors received a premium to all of them because if any one of them defaults then he has to make a payout to Bankers Trust."*

This enabled Bankers Trust to free up its credit lines to the Japanese financial sector. The main problem was to find investors willing to buy the notes. The incentive used was yield.

The market depends on two sets of counterparties – hedgers that wish to mitigate a particular credit risk and entities that want to assume that risk for a return. The BT notes paid a healthy spread over Libor of around 80bps to 100bps but investors faced coupon and principal losses if any of the institutions defaulted.

Sellers lead

The providers are largely investment banks. Much more than the commercial banks, they need the credit derivatives market to develop rapidly to enable them to manage the credit limits in their huge bond and derivative portfolios – particularly their riskier portfolios such as illiquid corporate and emerging market bonds.

Key point

> This way of selling credit risk has continued, and it is driven largely by the needs of the providers of the notes, not the buyers.

Investment banks need to manage these portfolios on a much more dynamic basis than the commercial banks do their loan portfolios because they have smaller balance sheets, their portfolios are marked to market daily and they tend to move in and out of fashionable sectors more quickly than syndicated lenders. They need to offload yesterday's risks in order to free up lines to carry on today's business.

But though investment banks will continue to exploit the potential of credit derivatives, the main users of the market – to begin with, at least – will be commercial banks. After five years of development the market has come up with standardized, priceable credit derivatives that commercial banks use.

Credit default swaps

Definition

> The building block of this category of credit derivatives is the credit default swap. A **credit default swap** is a bilateral financial contract in which one counterparty (the protection buyer) pays a periodic fee – typically expressed in fixed basis points on the notional amount – in return for a floating payment contingent on the default of one or

more third party reference credits. This floating payment is designed to mirror the loss incurred by creditors of the reference credit in the event of its default. It is usually calculated as the fall in price of a reference security that has defaulted.

Counterparties typically wait from one week to three months after default in order to give the price of the reference security time to settle at a new level.

Since most securities become due and payable in the event of default, most plain-vanilla securities will trade at the price that reflects the market's estimation of recovery following a default, irrespective of maturity or coupon.

Key point

This type of cash settled transaction was the most commonly used in the past. Now there are also structures in which there is physical delivery of the reference security, in particular default swaps, and this option of physical delivery is preferred.

One of the clearest applications of default swaps is the synthetic reallocation of credit risk between the loan and bond portfolios of the banks. Providers of the swaps envisage a liquid market in which financial institutions will use credit swaps to free lines filled up with loan transactions and bond and derivative portfolios. By paying another financial institution to take over the default risk on a loan or bond, or on a swap or option exposure to a single counterparty, banks can manage their credit limits quickly and confidentially, without having to undergo complex assignment procedures. This will enable banks, for the first time, to hedge the most difficult risks they face – concentration risk, correlation risk and the conflict between external regulatory and internal economic capital adequacy requirements.

Default swaps are the commonest type of credit derivative. They were the first to be applied to high quality credits and to be used for limit risk management and the elimination of risk on swap book exposures.

Example

Metro Bank, wishing to free up its credit lines to Italy at five years, enters into a five year default swap with an Italian government bond as the reference security. Metro pays a premium to the counterparty of, say, 20bps a year. The counterparty makes a payment in exchange only if Italy defaults on its debts, in which case the payment might be far less than the final price of the security, multiplied by the notional principal amount of the swap. In the simplest example, Metro Bank holds the same value of the underlying bond as the notional principal. So if Italy defaults, the reference bond falls to 85 per cent, Metro collects the 85 per cent from the market and the remaining 15 per cent from the swap counterparty. (See Figure 1.1.)

Fig 1.1

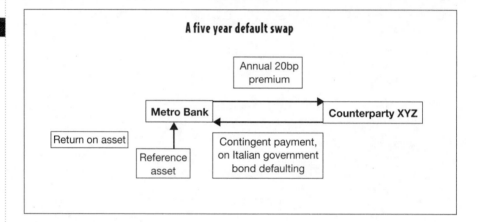

A five year default swap

Behind the borrower's back

In the above example, the fee of 20bps is not necessarily arrived at scientifically (see Chapter 8). Most likely it will have been determined by the spread to Libor that could be achieved by investing in comparable Italian securities. An arbitrage of sorts exists between the bond/asset swap market and the credit derivative market. No counterparty is likely to accept 20bps for assuming the default risk of a credit if it can take the same risk, by buying securities in the bond or asset swap markets, and receive Libor plus 30bps.

Another price check is the underlying cash position: you can think of a credit swap as equivalent to going long the risky bond and short the relevant (theoretical risk free) treasury.

However, if it can't take a similar position with a bond asset, the counterparty may be willing to accept less than 20bps for assuming the credit risk. There may be no other assets available from this credit; there may be assets available but not of the size or the maturity the counterparty requires; or the counterparty assuming the credit risk may be an institution that could never have participated in the original bond issue or syndicated loan either for relationship reasons or because its own funding costs are too high. Indeed, so fierce is competition in lending relationships at the moment that banks are building up portfolios of exposures to the key credits in the secondary loan and bond markets, the asset swap markets and the credit swap markets so that they can then approach these borrowers and pitch for relationship business on the basis of a significant existing commitment.

One man's meat ...

In the words of one banker: *"A bank will simply pay at the offer if it has too much exposure and will receive at the bid if it doesn't have enough. If the perceived market price for five year Fiat is 25bps mid, then a counterparty overexposed to Fiat is happy to pay 30bps in a default swap and a counterparty underexposed to Fiat is happy to receive at 15bps."*

> Transactions are often driven simply by their relative value to each counterparty.

Key point

These types of synthetic asset-reallocation trades are just as likely to involve strong credits as weak. The hedging institutions are not so much buying protection as using credit swaps to free credit lines in their loan or derivative portfolios and to reduce particular country exposures, so that they can do additional business. This is what stops the market from being completely one-sided. A market in which banks simply want to hedge would be characterized by long periods of inactivity and then frenzied one-way hedging as a credit sector moved visibly into problems.

Relationship banking

The credit default swap also enables banks to get credit risk off balance sheet where they might be obstructing higher margin business. For example, a key corporate client is looking for a large credit facility. He turns to his core relationship lenders, expecting them to take the bulk of the loan at razor thin margins. With limits pressed, the bank relationship managers must persuade ever more sceptical credit officers that the client's ancillary business will make up for the poor returns on the credit. At some point, no matter what the relationship, the concentration risk will be too great. On a risk-adjusted basis the loan is unprofitable and it is preventing other higher margin business from being done.

Selling a loan in the secondary market is of little use. Lesser institutions can use the secrecy of sub-participation or silent sub-participations to trade paper, but not the lead relationship banks.

A credit swap can solve the problem. The relationship bank subscribes to the loan but also enters a credit default swap agreement on the proportion of the loan it wishes to hedge. The borrower never knows that its relationship bank no longer holds the risk and so is happy to provide it with that additional high-margin business. If it's lucky, the relationship bank may even be able to exploit the current dearth of quality assets and make money on the default swap.

Corporate use of credit derivatives

It isn't only banks which can exploit the opportunities thrown up by credit derivatives. Now the mystery of their workings is starting to be unravelled, their scope is widening fast. Corporates, investors in projects, and insurance companies all stand to benefit.

Many customers are heavily exposed to a small number of key customers, e.g. an engineering company all of whose heavy drilling equipment in the next three years will be sold to a particular customer. In some areas of mining, where highly specialized equipment can take years to build and where two or three companies dominate a particular field, this is not unusual. If the customer goes bust, the manufacturer is left out of pocket holding machinery that no one else will buy. If the risk to its survival is serious enough it can now buy a credit default swap on a notional principal that gives it either the value of the machinery or some break-even amount.

Many customers are heavily exposed to a small number of key customers.

Then there is project finance. An equity sponsor to a large project may be happy with the operational and project risk but not the sovereign risk on the guarantees. It may have protected itself against 70 per cent of this risk via an export credit agency-backed facility. However it wants protection against the remaining 30 per cent. It could enter into a credit default swap with a notional principal equal to the amount not covered by the sovereign guarantee and with the same maturity so that, if the sovereign defaulted, it would receive the cash – *"The corporate sponsor might say, well we know the contracting company and are happy with the project risk but we are not happy about Indonesia. They will pay us a premium so that if Indonesia defaults, then we pay up,"* says one banker.

Hedging project risk

The only problem is that export credit agency (ECA) business is heavily subsidized and often banks cannot compete. However, the ECA guarantees are still modelled on matrices that have not changed to accommodate recent regional economic developments. The rates often reflect a time-warped view of the world.

At one time *"all the Asian economies were dreadful, so they charged a lot for guarantees to these countries,"* says one swapper. *"By contrast, the rates to Eastern European countries were low because they were a good risk as part of the Soviet empire. Now the economic situation has flipped, so we can't do much in Eastern Europe, but we can in Asia. Russia is ludicrously cheap but Thailand is ludicrously expensive."*

A company involved in a project that has a predictable payment stream can secure a more complex version of the project financing hedge. Credit swaps can be structured so that the company continues to receive the same payment stream in the event of default.

Employee remuneration

Another credit derivative structure protects employee remuneration. Where a group of employees is owed significant deferred compensation, they can pay a premium of a certain percentage of that future bonus pool to insure themselves against bankruptcy of their company. It doesn't take much imagination to see that such insurance is fraught with moral implications. The employees can bet their firm, knowing that the maximum downside for them is to be fired with their bonus intact.

Attractive as they seem, these risk management applications need counterparties willing to accept the credit risk. This is not straight-forward. Where it works best is the commercial banking sector with, ideally, counterparties which are large banks looking to swap concentration and concentration risks with other banks, or to arbitrage between different regional views of credit risk. But even between banks, such back-to-back trades are relatively rare. To find enough buyers to keep the market growing, banks have had to create enticing new structures, breaking down the underlying assets into parcels of credit risk which alter the maturities and the leverage. The most straight-forward of these trades involves swaps used to create synthetic assets that do not exist in the markets. The market can fail to supply investment opportunities in the required maturities, or the constraints on the maximum term of an investment fund may restrict investment in credits which only issue longer maturities.

For example, a bank might have a two year line for a credit that issues only five year debt – a credit swap can be tailored to create a synthetic two year asset indexed to the default risk of the five year cash asset. A bank might have a five year line but be full out to the second year; a forward-start credit swap could also enable an investor to benefit from wide forward credit spreads without having to go long one asset and short the other.

On the other side of these trades are hedgers wanting either to hedge just part of an exposure – rather than liquidate an entire position – or to hedge an exposure for a limited period. A credit swap's notional principal and maturity can be tailored to provide exactly the amount and tenor of protection required.

Balance sheets to rent

The more complex credit swaps take into account basis risk between the payout formula of the swap and the actual loss incurred by the hedger. In a credit swap on a bond, the payment to the hedger on default is based on a bid for the reference bond. If the bid does not accurately reflect its exposure – perhaps because the swap valuation is made one month after default but subsequent events push the final recovery value much lower – then swaps can be created that pay out a fixed percentage of par which the hedger believes will mirror its loss. This in turn is usually based on historical data for the maturity, rating and security type. It is generally difficult for intermediaries to place risk based on this kind of formula and so it tends to be expensive and time-consuming.

In these cases counterparties must take particular views of likely recovery rates.

Key point

> Any counterparty asked to take fixed recovery must judge whether that percentage is fair, given any available data and also given the market pricing of any outstanding debt.

More complex adjustments to the payout on default can create first loss/second loss restructuring of a credit and plays on the actual recovery of the credit.

In the more complex credit derivative structures, an increasing amount of credit responsibility is adopted by the counterparty. In some structures even the new counterparty risk arising from the credit derivative is laid off.

The workings of a total return swap

The total return credit swap, first seen about three years ago, not only pays a premium to the counterparty assuming the default risk, it also periodically marks to market the underlying loan or bond.

The holder of a loan with positive carry pays all cash flows from the loan – Libor plus spread and all fees – to the swap counterparty. In exchange, the counterparty pays Libor back to the bank. Periodically the swap is settled on the market value of the loan. Any positive change in value is paid by the premium payer (the bank) to the default risk holder (the swap counterparty). Any negative change is paid by the default risk holder to the premium payer. (See Chapter 2.)

The bank paying the premium in this kind of swap is effectively warehousing a loan, renting out its balance sheet while transferring the economic value of the loan to a third party. The motivation behind this type of transaction is a need to get rid of an asset without entering a physical transaction that might upset the borrower.

But what if the receiving counterparty is as risky as the loan being warehoused? There is little point in, say, Lehman Brothers offloading an exposure to a strong single-A rated sovereign credit if the swap counterparty is a weak single-A. Even if the risk being sold is BB, the effect of the sale is seriously diluted by the counterparty risk.

Worse still, there is a correlation issue. If an investment bank wishes to lay off Belgian sovereign risk, then the effect on its own overall credit risk portfolio will be different depending on whether it sells that risk to a counterparty whose fortunes are linked to those of the Belgian economy or to one whose are not. Sell to a Belgian bank and the probability is that a sovereign default will cause problems in the banking sector. Better to sell to an Asian bank unlikely to be affected by a European economic crisis. The problem is, first, to evaluate the exact probability of joint default so that the net post-swap credit exposure can be worked out and, second, to find enough uncorrelated counterparties interested in or knowledgeable about the credit risk that has to be sold.

Working out the net credit effect of a swap and examining every counterparty in turn is not practical. One solution is a credit linked note. By selling a note whose principal and coupon are linked to default events, the seller of the risk has no exposure to the institution that assumes the default risk. In the event of default, the buyer of the notes simply gets less principal back or a lower coupon.

The structured credit linked note market

Structured notes are always more expensive and less liquid than the under-lying components. This is all the more true of credit linked notes where the lack of standardized documentation – the International Swaps and Derivatives Association is negoti-ating what one banker terms 'a bid/offer spread in the language' – and the attendant risks might result in a legal nightmare. Also, most structured note buyers tend to be credit neutral: they are prepared to take very significant market risk as long as there is a triple-a (AAA) or double-a (AA) note underlying the trade.

The structured credit linked note market has concentrated on weaker, particularly emerging, market credits and complex range and spread trades.

Traditional fixed-income investors are neither volume buyers of structured notes nor are they easy to persuade to take credit risk.

Finding investors for this paper, therefore, requires very high yield, a singular view of the risks involved and a sales approach that emphasizes the ability to take sophisticated views difficult or impossible to express in the cash markets.

Transactions will be driven by investors:

- looking at spreads;
- looking at relative perceptions of credit;
- looking to strip credit risk from other instruments so as to play it; and
- wishing to take views on credit that cannot be expressed with existing instruments.

For example, at the moment, there is very little single-a (A) paper available and any that there is, is quickly snapped up in the asset swap market. Using credit swaps enables us to provide investors with ex-posure to this sector.

Providing yields high enough after structuring costs to entice investors has tested the ingenuity of note sellers even though the risks they want to lay off are already high yield. The structured credit linked note market has concentrated on weaker, particularly emerging, market credits and complex range and spread trades. The focus in such a situation is on finding buyers for difficult credits so that clients, one of which is usually the bank's own internal credit risk management department, can be offered protection against them.

Some worrying trends in the credit linked note market

The investment banks cannot warehouse anything like the volume that commercial banks can: *"We could warehouse smaller transactions, say $25 million to $50 million, in the same way we could take on that kind of bond position,"* says one swapper. *"However, for larger deals, we have to find a buyer for the risk and so we depend on our distribution network."*

The simplest credit linked note embeds a credit swap in a fixed income instrument. In return for an enhanced yield – the premium paid under the swap less the investment bank's cut – the investor accepts a redemption formula with the potential for loss of principal or coupon should a particular borrower default. This loss mirrors that on the underlying swap, which is the difference between par and the price of a reference security. Assuming that some recovery will take place, the loss will be limited.

But there is one note structure which worries even those who provide it, and some banks refuse to sell it at all. To increase yields further, some banks market a product known as the zero-one structure. Here, instead of some coupon and principal loss, investors lose all their principal if there is a default.

The problem with such a structure is that there just aren't that many fixed income assets that become worthless on one trigger event. It is a headache waiting to happen – when somebody loses (which they haven't yet).

According to lawyers who have worked on these deals, even the banks that sell them – which include CSFP, Morgan Stanley – devote extra time to the legal documents to ensure there are no misunderstandings of the terms. Paranoia is too strong a word, but the banks realize that even one client able to claim it didn't understand it could lose everything would lead to costly litigation.

The kind of yields available depend on the assumed recovery rate of the reference asset. If an investor could receive a premium of 100bps on an assumed recovery rate of 50 per cent, then a zero-one structure would double that.

Betting on bankruptcy

The difficulty with the zero-one structure is that you have to be absolutely certain that the reference asset will not default. But you can't be absolutely certain – that's like saying the reference credit is risk free, so why is the market demanding a premium to lend to it?

What is happening here is that people whose own default is highly correlated with that of the reference asset are buying these notes. For example, a small Korean bank is happy to take this trade on Korea Development Bank (KDB) because if KDB is bust, then so are they. So a loss on the note is irrelevant.

Basket trades

Basket trades have also become popular.

> **Definition**
>
> In a **basket trade,** instead of the swap being referenced to just one credit, it is referenced to a basket. If any one of the credits in the basket defaults, the swap counterparty must pay the specified default amount.

In this way, you can buy an asset swap and sell someone else – usually the dealer – the right to put you into any one of, say, three other credits on specified dates. The dealer will only exercise that right if it can substitute a cheap bond for an expensive one. Such an option is not priced theoretically but according to what its worth is to the individual counterparty. The dealer may have a view on a particular bond and the investor, or if it does not have to mark to market, it may be indifferent as to which of the bonds it holds as long as none are downgraded below a particular floor.

The next step is to tailor notes more precisely to the investors' requirements by designing a credit swap whose maturity or other terms do not match those of the underlying security. Emerging market sovereign plays are popular.

Credit spread plays

An investor may wish to take a six month exposure to Brazil when the shortest maturity paper available is twice that. A note can be structured with a six month credit swap embedded so that the investor is exposed to Brazil's default risk only for the six month period required. On the other side of the trade, the investment bank, or an end client, is looking to hedge Brazilian risk for just six months, perhaps in anticipation of a particular event or just to reduce pressure on the Brazil country limit.

One popular emerging market trade involves the most liquid securities. There is a misconception that you can use credit derivatives to strip out sovereign risk from emerging market bonds. There is no value in doing that unless you can find investors with wildly different views on the credit. Much more popular have been trades that restructure the cash flows on emerging market securities or that strip out the US treasury risk from Brady bonds.

The most complex trades focus on the yield difference between credit sensitive instruments and reference government bonds. Assuming that fixed income instruments of the same duration move together in price as interest rates change, the main reason for any changes in spread is a changed perception of credit risk. So options on the credit spread allow investors to isolate credit risk from interest rate risk.

Key point

- The purchaser of a credit spread call will profit if spreads tighten.
- The purchaser of a put will profit if spreads widen.
- Sell a credit spread put and, as long as spreads do not widen to the strike, the premium is profit.
- Sell a call and, as long as they do not tighten to the strike, the premium is profit.

As with any option, buying and selling credit spread options means taking a view on credit spread volatility. This is generally much higher yield volatility, because lags between moves in the treasury market and in the non-government bond market mean that there is imperfect correlation between the two.

Spread options

As with credit swaps, spread options allow investors to take credit views whose duration is different from that of the underlying reference instrument. These views can be leveraged – a 1bp move in the underlying spread produces a 2bps, 3bps or even 5bps move in the value of the option to further customize the spread risk of any note in which the option is embedded. Also, as with swaps, the options do not need to be cash settled. The holder of a physically settled put would have a right to deliver an underlying bond to the option counterparty at a predetermined price if its spread rose to a particular level.

> **Spread options** are priced off the credit spread curve, off expected volatility and expected recovery. This tells you what probability of default is implied in the option price. Default probability does not drive pricing.

Stripping Bradys

Bradys (rescheduled sovereign debt packaged into bonds whose principal is backed by long-dated US treasury zero-coupon bonds) are the most popular instruments for investing in emerging markets because of their liquidity and because their long maturities give better potential for profiting from the improvement of the sovereign credit.

However, the US treasury collateral gives investors double exposure – to the emerging country's sovereign risk and to US dollar interest rate risk. So any rise in the price of a Brady bond, due to improved credit perceptions, may be offset by rising US interest rates.

Despite the fact that traders often quote Bradys in terms of stripped yield, i.e. the yield on the non-US dollar portion of the bond, constructing the appropriate interest rate hedge to gain exposure only on the sovereign risk component is complex. Even experts disagree on the best methodology.

Credit spread options are the answer. Investors can now buy options on the credit spread of the liquid Brady bonds over US treasuries, leaving bank traders to create the Brady bonds/US treasury position that hedges such options. A call on the Brazil spread over treasuries would profit if spreads tighten (Brazil's credit improves) and a put would profit if spreads widen.

This trade gives investors easy access to the stripped yield spread over treasuries which is the best measurement of the sovereign's credit quality and which should move independently of US interest rates in a way that Bradys themselves do not.

A similar concept, that of stripping one risk from another, has applied to corporate debt. Investors have been offered options on the spread between a corporate security and the debt of the country in which the corporate is domiciled. The investor gains exposure to the corporate credit risk but not the underlying sovereign. Banks have even offered options on the spread between a company's senior and subordinated debt.

Getting round guidelines

If a particular issuer's bonds are trading at a high historical credit spread, investors can buy calls on the spread, or notes that pay an above market return as long as the spread stays within the bands implied by the recent spread volatility that has pushed the spreads so high.

> Credit options can be used to take views on the volatility of credit spreads.

Key point

As with many other highly structured notes, assets with these types of options embedded can be used by asset managers to circumvent restrictions on their portfolios. A one year floating rate note could be constructed for a money market fund manager that incorporated the purchase of a call on the credit spread of a five year bond and the sale of a put on that spread. The investor believes that spreads will tighten and so buys the call at the present spread of 150bps over treasuries and sells the put out-of-the-money at, say, 200bps over. Though he is not normally allowed to buy five year bonds, he benefits from any tightening of five year credit spreads (and losses if spreads widen significantly). Since the note is below his duration barrier he has not broken the rules governing his portfolio.

Bankers argue that the exact duration of the underlying security is not important since the recovery rate on a defaulted two year note is the same as that on a ten year bond – a two year swap on a ten year paper is a two year credit risk. It is not clear how many investors' internal guidelines will cope with notes whose performance is linked to forward credit spreads. The rating agencies provide some guidance but the scope for abuse remains.

Binary structures have also been created. Investors can purchase notes that pay a significantly enhanced yield as long as the credit spread does not trade outside a specified range at any time. If it does, the yield is substantially below prevailing market rates. Generally the boundaries specified are the minimum and maximum levels the bond traded in a predetermined period.

Other trades have seen investors sell another counterparty the right to swap them from one security into one of a specified group of different securities, if a particular credit spread level is breached. (In other words, swap out currents in the security position to another position comprising the basket of securities, providing a particular spread level is breached on the existing position.)

Example

Investor A, the holder of a sovereign bond, believes the bond's spread to a reference treasury will remain stable at 55bps. Investor A decides to enhance its return by selling an option; the holder of the option can swap investor A into another security of the same rating, either specified or chosen from a specified basket, if the spread tightens below 40bps. If this does happen, the option holder will obviously swap investor A into a cheaper bond and take the expensive security, pocketing the difference.

Ratings-based derivatives

New ratings-based derivatives, and instruments based on credit and loan indices, will help bondholders hedge against credit migration. You might expect derivatives based on ratings to be the most popular, but right now one trade a year is about the average for the banks that do them.

Key point

One large credit derivative market of the future will be the provision of instruments that are hedged not against default risk, but against ratings changes.

These instruments break down the transition from today until default into a series of movements or notches – the credit ratings. The difficulty in creating them is pricing the credit migration that will take place in a year or other period.

One problem is that there is no stable relationship between rating and spread, i.e. securities with the same rating trade differently. So a derivative that protects an investor against the drop from single-a (A) to triple-b (BBB) cannot be expressed either as a simple credit spread option or as an option to switch from one security to another – both would normally be priced off the credit spread curve. "*It is very hard to model a subjective event rather than an economic event,*" says one swapper. "*Though the agencies would disagree, ratings still depend on the mood of an analyst at a particular time. We cannot price something that depends on the action of one guy or a small number of people.*"

Another difficulty is that most of the investors desiring this trade would be fund managers protecting themselves against a drop in ratings that would take a security below their rating floor. It is hard to see who would be on the other side of the trade.

The difficulty is compounded by the fact that credit has traditionally been priced off default. Because loans have not traditionally been marked to market, there is little data on the sensitivity of portfolios to change in the credit quality of individual assets within them; and so there is no way for individual lenders or investors to put a value on an instrument that hedges them against downgrades. In any case, this value would depend almost entirely on the concentration and correlation risk in their portfolios. So even if loan officers were sensitive to downgrades, it's unlikely that a bank would take the other side of the trade because it wouldn't be able to price the risk to its portfolio of the trade.

Just the beginning

The majority of fixed income fund managers buy only investment grade bonds and maintain a credit buffer between the weakest bonds in their portfolio and the level at which they must sell.

This is why in Europe strong single-a (A) tends to be the minimum acceptable rating: a credit warning doesn't force an immediate fire sale. That makes fund managers very unlikely to take a trade that puts them into a security below their floor. One possibility is a transatlantic arbitrage: the floor for many US fund managers is triple-b (BBB). They might accept a trade in which they were paid for the risk of being put into a weak single-a (A) or strong triple-b (BBB) security.

Scarcity of data means that trends in ratings changes are difficult to analyze.

Scarcity of data means that trends in ratings changes are difficult to analyze. For example, it's clear that there are more downgrades than upgrades and that prices fall more when an entity is downgraded than they rise if it is upgraded. But much more data and analysis is needed to formulate rules that could help price these types of instrument.

Hedges against ratings changes and options on the credit spread between similar fixed-income instruments lie at the more esoteric end of the product spectrum. Their widespread usage is still in the future, but it is a future that is approaching rapidly and with plain-vanilla products has already arrived.

The market for credit derivatives

The market for credit derivatives is definitely a growing market, in 1995–6 the notional volume of deals outstanding has grown from something like $5 billion to more than $50 billion, according to JP Morgan. See the introduction on credit derivatives for a 1997–8 update on credit derivative volumes. This is almost two-thirds of the $75 billion structured note market, in terms of annual new issuance. In London a dealer survey estimates that there are $200 billion outstanding CDs. The number is estimated to grow to $200 billion notional credit derivative transactions by the year 2000. Compared to global OTC, derivatives are at $47 trillion.

The credit derivative market is experiencing growing pains. Buyers of credit protection are often hard to find. There is little transparency in the way deals are priced and the market is shallow and illiquid when a hedge is required or to unwind trades. Regulators have not finished working on the issues within the context of capital adequacy rulings.

The players

Credit derivatives have been the preserve of the large Wall Street firms, e.g. Bankers Trust, Chase Manhattan, and JP Morgan. However, Swiss and German banks are now following suit, e.g. UBS, DMG, and Dresner Kleinwort Benson. Finally, even the Japanese banks are entering into the picture, e.g. Nomura.

There are difficulties in assessing the size of the market. The Bank for International Settlements (BIS) and the International Swaps and Derivatives Association (ISDA) do not collect turnover figures for the credit market; also certain banks define credit derivatives differently.

Summary

Just as interest rate derivatives were destined for success because they allowed investors to separate and restructure interest rate risk, so the ability to separate credit risk from an underlying financial instrument guarantees the market's success.

Credit derivatives are also redefining the relationship between the supply and demand for credit. Traditionally, credit was sourced in the new issue market and placed with end investors. But now it is possible to unbundle credit risk from loans, bonds and swaps and place it in a different form into different markets.

Key point

> For the risk manager, credit derivatives offer an important means of stripping out credit risk from market risk. For the institutional investor, they represent a new asset class with potentially very high returns.

Credit Derivative Instruments

Introduction

The principal feature of credit derivative instruments is that they separate and isolate credit risk allowing the trading of credit risk with the purpose of:

- replicating credit risk
- transferring credit risk
- hedging credit risk.

The principal products, usually referred to as credit derivative instruments, are:

- *Credit default products* – default swaps, credit default options, indemnity agreements.
- *Total rate of return swaps* – (also known as loan swaps).
- *Credit spread products* – credit spread options, forwards.

The market for credit derivatives is segmented between the following sectors:

- investment grade credits
- non-investment grade/high yield credits
- distressed credit assets
- emerging market credits.

This chapter focus primarily on credit default swaps and total rate of return swaps which are dealt with in depth. A brief overview of credit options will conclude the chapter. Credit linked notes are dealt with in Chapter 4, and collaterized mortgage obligations are covered in Chapter 6.

1 Credit default swaps

In this section we look at those credit derivative instruments collectively known as credit default products: in particular, the credit default swap.

> **Credit default products** are products that isolate the risk on credit obligations.

Definition

The exact structure of these products is often regulation or jurisdiction driven. However, the main elements are common to all forms of the transaction. The underlying default risk that is to be traded can be defined to a high level: static exposures (such as bonds or loans) and dynamic exposures (such as those occurring in market value driven instruments, primarily derivatives like interest rate swaps) can then be separated and passed to another counterparty.

All obligations or a nominated subset of credit assets of the issuer can be identified. This categorization may be by seniority of debt or by market issue (bank versus bond/public markets).

The instrument can be linked to an individual credit or a basket of credits to create a specified or diversified exposure to default risk.

The transfer of default risk

A credit default swap enables the transfer of default risk. The bank pays a premium, typically expressed as a certain number of basis points per annum on the nominal of the contract, and a payment is only due to the bank if there is a credit event by the reference credit. A credit event is bankruptcy, insolvency, or a payment default: the contingent payment may be the purchase of a defaulted asset at par, or such a transfer may be cash settled.

The bank has effectively purchased a default hedge, the investor secures a spread taking an off balance sheet credit exposure. For the less liquid reference credits, the purchase of a defaulted asset is not practical and, in the absence of a good proxy for the recovery rate of the reference credit, the parties to the transaction must pre-agree the contingent payment. In this structure, often referred to as a 'binary' transaction, the investor commits to pay this pre-agreed amount following a credit event.

Reference credit

The default of the reference credit triggers the contingent payout. The reference credit must be nominated under the default swap contract. Individual or basket credit structures are possible.

Reference credit asset

The relevant credit asset issued by the reference credit must be specified under the default swap contract. All or a specific subset of obligations may be chosen. The price of the asset must be agreed at the commence-

Credit default swap

Fig 2.1

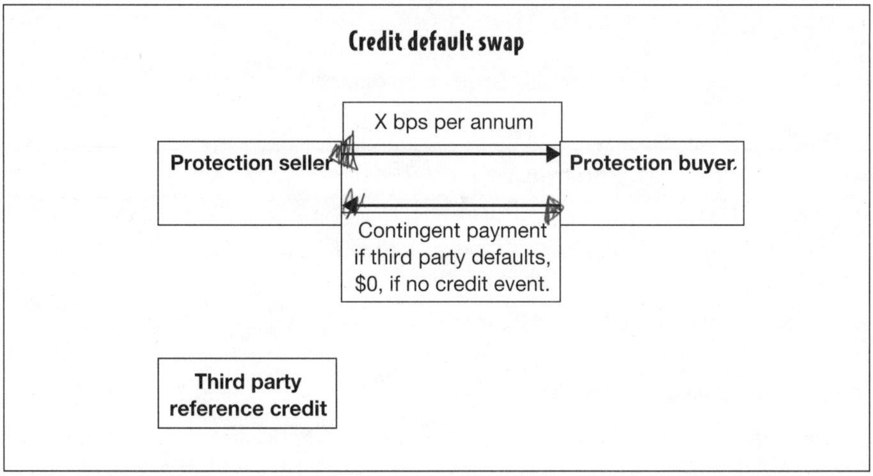

ment of the transaction. This is particularly important where the default payment is based on the post default price of the security.

What is meant by a credit event?

The definition of default varies from bank to bank and from trade to trade. The credit event triggers the obligation of the provider of default protection to make the default payment to the purchaser of default protection.

A credit event can be:

- bankruptcy
- insolvency
- restructuring, administration or Chapter 11 or equivalent bankruptcy protection filing by the issuer
- failure to meet a payment obligation when due
- rating downgrade below agreed threshold
- change in credit spread above agreed level.

Most trades include a 'materiality' clause calling for significant price movements in the reference credit bond or stock.

Most trades include a 'materiality' clause calling for significant price movements in the reference credit bond or stock. This prevents the swap from triggering unjustifiably if, for example, the reference credit omits a payment with one of its bankers since it disputes the legality of a contract.

What is the fee or premium?

The fee earned by the protection seller depends on the:

- maturity of the trade
- probability of the reference party going into default
- credit rating of the swap counterparty
- relationship 'correlation' between the reference credit and the swap counterparty
- expected recovery value of the reference asset.

Maturity of the trade

Long maturity trades command more fees, because the seller takes on a lot more risk and it is harder to estimate this risk.

Probability of default

The more probable default is, the higher the fees. A good proxy is Moody's or S&P's credit ratings (see Table 2.1). Big derivative houses compute their own 'probability of default'.

Credit rating of the protection seller

There is no point in substituting a reference party's credit rating with a lower rated swap counterparty. Subject to correlation, a bank which is rated BBB might be tempted to write as much protection as it can on an AAA name. If the AAA name defaults it is quite likely, given some degree of correlation, that the bank will also default, so why not write the protection and earn the premium.

So you wouldn't want to buy protection on an AAA credit from a BBB bank. On the other hand, if you buy protection on a BB name you would pay more for a swap with an AAA counterparty than a swap with an A counterparty. You are paying more for higher quality protection.

The contingent leg or the default payment

The contingent payment depends on the losses actually incurred by the protection buyer in case the reference credit goes into default. It can be the fall in price of a benchmark floating rate bond a few months after the default event. The question that now needs to be answered is how much below par did it fall?

Key point

> Swaps can be settled either in cash or through delivery of the underlying asset.

Table 2.1 Summary of corporate bond ratings systems and symbols

Moody's	S&P	Fitch	Brief definition
Investment grade: High creditworthiness			
Aaa	AAA	AAA	Gilt-edge, prime, maximum safety
Aa1	AA+	AA+	
Aa2	AA	AA	Very high grade, high quality
Aa3	AA–	AA–	
A1	A+	A+	
A2	A	A	Upper medium grade
A3	A–	A–	
Baa1	BBB+	BBB+	
Baa2	BBB	BBB	Lower medium grade
Baa3	BBB–	BBB–	
Distinctly speculative: Low creditworthiness			
Ba1	BB+	BB+	
Ba2	BB	BB	Low grade, speculative
Ba3	BB–	BB–	
B1	B+	B+	
B2	B	B	Highly speculative
B3	B–	B–	
Predominantly speculative: Substantial risk or in default			
Caa	CCC+ CCC CCC–	CCC	Substantial risk
Ca	CC	CC	May be in default
C	C	C	
	CI		Income bonds, no interest is being paid
		DDD	Default
		|DD	
	D	D	

This is not done until two or three months after default to give the market time to estimate the 'recovery value'. The recovery value of a reference asset defines how much of the debt is recovered after default.

To summarize, there are three methods of payment, of which the third listed is the most widely used:

1 Notional principal *(1 or initial price – post default price of reference security, as determined by dealer poll or from price quote services). Typically up to five dealers are polled bi-weekly over a one to three month period following default or the credit event and the results averaged.

2 Pre-agreed fixed percentage of notional principal (notional principal is typically $25 million to $50 million).

3 Payment of par or initial price by default protection provider in exchange for delivery of defaulted credit asset.

Credit default swap cash flows

Common to a standard swap, the present value of default swaps is zero upon origination. Cash flows and not principal, are exchanged between two counterparties. These cash flows depend on the term of the swap and the underlying reference credit. The 'protection buyer' purchases credit protection and is short the credit exposure. The 'protection seller' sells credit protection and is long the credit exposure.

Key point

> The swap quote is dependent on the periodic premium payment made to the protection seller.

The protection seller receives a stream of payments from the protection buyer. These payments are referred to as premium and are paid quarterly, in arrears, on an actual/360 day calendar. The premium, expressed in basis points per annum over the swap tenor, is also the swap quote. This type of cash flow structure is similar to other types of swaps.

Key point

> The cash flow paid to the protection buyer, in contrast, is unique to default swaps.

The protection buyer's 'cash flow' is contingent on the occurrence of a default event, as well as the payout specified in the swap agreement.

As Figure 2.1 shows, the protection buyer will receive nothing if a credit event does not occur. In the swap documentation, the definition of a credit event is consistent with standard default nomenclature. Generally, the following events denote default: failure to pay a scheduled interest or principal payment; bankruptcy or insolvency; receivership; and acceleration of pari passu credits.

Default swap settlement

Default swap payout structures have evolved with the market. Early swap agreements were cash settled, whereas today a majority of corporate and sovereign default swaps are physically settled.

In the standard cash settled swap, payments to the buyer of protection are calculated by multiplying the notional amount of the swap by the difference between par and the market price of the defaulted asset, frequently stated as notional * (max[100 – $P_{default}$,0]). The price of the defaulted bond ($P_{default}$) is the price of the reference asset upon default and is usually established by a polling of secondary market bids. Another type of cash settlement is a binary payout, where ($P_{default}$) or the recovery price is predetermined in the agreement. For example, a binary payout of notional * (max[100 – 50%,0]) is based on a fixed recovery price of 50 per cent of par.

> *Default swap payout structures have evolved with the market. Early swap agreements were cash settled, whereas today a majority of corporate and sovereign default swaps are physically settled.*

The economics of cash and physical settlement are the same

Physical settlement has become increasingly standard. In this case, the protection buyer has the right to put the defaulted reference obligation to the protection seller for par. The 'payment' to the buyer of protection is effectively par versus the delivery of a defaulted asset. Conceptually, the economics of both types of settlements should be the same. However, investors' concerns associated with cash settled swaps have led to the trend toward physical settlement. Most notably, immediately after a credit event, an asset's price can be volatile, the market is illiquid and pricing may not be reliable. Physical settlement can protect both parties from flaws in price discovery.

A physical payout is designed to mirror the 'loss' on an obligation of the reference credit in the event of default, assuming the reference asset was purchased for par. For the protection seller, physical settlement will mimic the experience of a holder of the actual cash asset of the reference credit should a credit event occur. The seller may choose to hold the defaulted asset through the bankruptcy process. Conversely, the protection buyer is usually a hedger who owns an asset of the reference credit and, upon default, can simply deliver the asset for par.

Reference credits and deliverable obligations

The reference asset can take several forms. It can be a marketable security, such as a public bond issued by the reference credit, a revolving line of credit, a bank loan, a swap obligation, a trade receivable, or classes of assets within the capital structure. Following a credit event, if physical settlement is the payout mechanism, swap contracts allow for rights of substitution of pari passu obligations. The reason for this is the defaulted assets of a creditor are fungible. Specifically, as the debt obligations of a defaulted issuer have equivalent present values, *any* debt obligation of equivalent priority of the defaulted creditor can be delivered to the protection seller.

In most contracts these assets must meet specific characteristics such as bearing simple interest which is paid in a specific currency.

Key point

> Default swaps increase the breadth of the credit market.

The embedded credit risk in a swap is a function of the term of the swap. This means that a specific credit risk can be not only customized into an exposure that does not exist in the cash market, but also consolidated into a single swap contract. For example, a three year default swap could be structured on a credit that only had longer-term bonds outstanding; thus, filling a hole in the credit curve. I believe that, over time, default swaps will lead to more complete pricing in the cash market because they allow for all points along an issuer's credit curve to be traded.

Early termination and assignability

Like other types of swaps, credit default swaps can be terminated prior to term. Although default swaps are not freely transferable, investors can terminate the swap early at the current market value of the swap with the original counterparty. If counterparties agree to terminate the swap, they can either: terminate the swap with the original counterparty at current market prices; or assign the swap to another acceptable counterparty.

Key point

> Assignability allows each counterparty the flexibility to effectively terminate the swap exposure with counterparties other than the original counterparty at the most competitive price.

Some credit default swap trade examples

Basic credit default swap

A typical credit default swap quote is presented in Table 2.2. The swap represents four year protection on Ford Motor Company, the largest issuer in the investment grade corporate index. This is an actively traded credit in the credit derivatives market, since corporate bond underwriters and banks frequently need protection in this name to hedge both secondary bond, loan and swap counterparty exposures.

Example

Table 2.2 Default swap quote: Ford Motor Company (A1/A)

Term	Bid	Offer	Ref obligation
4yrs	45	55	F 7.25% 10/1/08

Payout/Settlement
Physical, Par versus
delivery, 8 October 1998

(Currency Ford 4x 29/35 – June 1999)

In this swap, the underlying reference asset is a ten year debenture, the F 7.25% 10/1/08. The swap is quoted at 45/55bps: protection is offered at 55bps and bid at 45bps. (For simplicity we will assume this cash flow is paid annually.) A protection seller would receive 45bps per annum on the notional amount for providing protection to the buyer for four years. For instance, in a $25 million transaction, the seller would receive $114,063 (0.0045 * 365/360 * $25,000,000) each year, over the life of the swap. In the event of default, the agreement would terminate and the seller would pay $25 million times par in exchange for the delivery of the defaulted bond.

The maximum total payment received by the protection seller is $456,250, the sum of the individual premium payments. Assuming the delivered debt obligation is worth 50 cents on the dollar following a credit event, the maximum loss for the protection provider is $12,500,000. If the credit defaulted in the third year, as shown in Figure 2.2, the protection seller would have cash flows equal to ($228,125 + accrual on the swap premium payment – $12,5000,000). Note that these types of payouts are typical of events that have low frequency and high severity, such as default events.

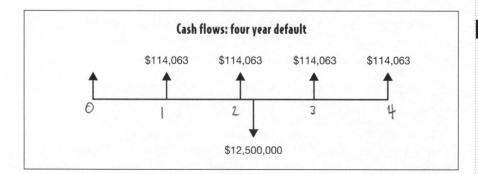

Cash flows: four year default

$114,063 $114,063 $114,063 $114,063

$12,500,000

Fig 2.2

Early termination and swap market value

Assuming that the protection seller chose to terminate or assign the swap in one year, the total cash flow of the swap would equate to the premium cash flow, accrued interest and the change in the market value of the swap. The change in the market value of the swap is approximately the change in the swap premium (in basis points) times the risk factor (the dollar value of a basis point of an annuity stream with a maturity equal to the remaining maturity of the swap agreement). In the case of the Ford swap in the example above, assume the swap was terminated at the end of the first year and the market for three year protection on Ford was 20/25. The price change in the swap would be approximately $0.54. This amount represents 20bps of 'spread tightening' times the 0.270 dollar value of a basis point for three year cash flow.

An investor hedging exposure to default by a given reference credit

A very simple application of a credit default swap is when an investor owns a particular bond and would like to protect himself from any possibility of default, without wanting to sell the bond.

Assume, investors who owned long maturity bonds issued by a company (XYZ Company). The issuer's bonds have seen a widening of credit spreads with three year spreads currently quoted at 115bps and 12 year spreads at 203bps. The investor could, if concerned with shorter-term default risk, hedge with the following credit default swap:

Maturity of default swap: three years
Reference credit: XYZ Company
Reference bond: XYZ Company 8.50% three year bond

Credit event: On the first business day following a default on its senior debt or a bankruptcy filing by the reference credit.

Default payment: Notional amount * [100% – fair market value of reference bond after default]
Default swap premium: 3.20% (flat) payable by the entity purchasing protection
Payment of default payment: The default payment is payable by the entity providing protection upon the occurrence of a credit event.

The transaction would have allowed the investor to hedge its exposure to default by the reference credit. An investor purchasing the underlying 12 year bond could have hedged its default risk for the first 3 years and still enjoyed a positive spread on the reference credit's 12 year bonds of around 80bps over treasuries.

Basket linked credit default swap

In a basket linked credit deposit swap, credit default is based on a basket of underlying assets with different issuers.

> The important issue is the concept of first to default. So the credit event that triggers the default payment or physical settlement with respect to the underlying asset is the first default of any of the credit assets included in the basket of credits.

Key point

The combination of credit risks in the basket linked credit default swap creates a lower credit quality than the individual credit standing of the credit assets. This reflects, primarily, the combination of two factors: the low default correlation between the credit assets included in the basket and the fact that there is an element of inherent leverage in the structure (in a US$50 million transaction on four underlying credit assets – a five year German bond, five year Swiss bond, five year Danish bond and a five year French bond – the provider of default protection, because it provides protection on any of the four assets up to a face value of US$50 million on a first to default basis, is providing protection on US$200 million of credit assets).

Receivers of default protection

In practice, the first of these structures to be traded had high quality underlying credit assets such as European sovereign issuers. The motivation for this type of trade was the need for active commercial and investment banks to hedge large concentrations of credit exposures to these European countries. This primarily related to capital market activity, such as interest rate swaps, currency swaps and standby credit facilities in order to support funding of these borrowers, and limits to facilitate trading in securities issued by these entities.

Providers of default protection

Providers of protection under these structures are primarily institutional investors seeking higher yields on high quality securities. The higher yield obtained on these first to default baskets is attractive to investors who did not properly quantify the additional marginal risk of the structure or who were indifferent to the risks, as the underlying credit assets were eligible investments for these investors on a standalone purchase basis.

Far Eastern investors, including Japanese institutions, and European and Middle Eastern investors were initially the main providers of these types of credit default protection. The attraction of these structures from the perspective of the parties purchasing protection, was that these structures enabled them to reduce large credit concentrations within their portfolios at an attractive cost. Recently the structure has been used primarily with Japanese banks and emerging market credits. The emergence of significant credit problems within the Japanese banking system in the middle 1990s prompted a significant volume of transaction which primarily entailed the sale of default risk on the weaker Japanese financial institutions through these first to default credit structures. The driving force was the necessity to reduce the large credit concentrations within bank portfolios to this group of obligors. The protection was provided by Far Eastern investors, including better capitalized Japanese financial institutions, primarily institutional investors, as well as investors in other markets with low levels of exposure to Japanese bank risk.

Providers of protection under these structures are primarily institutional investors seeking higher yields on high quality securities.

The emerging market transaction involved trading baskets of Latin, South-East Asian and, more recently, Eastern European risk. The underlying rationale of these transactions was for large international money centre commercial and investment banks active in these markets to diversify or trade out of large risk concentration to particular counterparties to allow them to continue to transact business with these counterparties. The providers of default protection were again institutional investors willing to take the default risk to these issuers/counterparties.

In all these types of transactions, a major driving force was the fact that the format of the transfer of credit risk created in these first to default baskets was attractive for the investors assuming the default risk. The structures embedded in notes/securities provided an elegant mechanism for creating the desired exposure while allowing the investors to generate incremental yields which provide outperformance relative to the underlying benchmarks against which the performance of these investors was measured.

The two issues that, in practice, create the greatest difficulties are the definition of the event of default and the calculation of default payment. These issues impact not only on credit default swaps but also, as noted above, on total return loan swaps (the loan value must be calculated periodically).

In practice the definition of default usually combines a trigger event, the existence of public information regarding the credit event, and, increasingly, the concept of materiality.

The concept of materiality is based on a minimum change in either the price of the bond or loan or in the spread of the bond or loan relative to a benchmark rate. This provision is designed to ensure that there has been a true credit event triggering the requirement to make the default payment and to avoid the possibility of triggering a credit event when there has not, in reality, been an event of default.

The calculation of default payment presents greater problems. The fixed payout structure is the only default mechanism which is relatively free of doubt.

Basket linked credit default swap

Example

Counterparties: [Dealer] and [Investor]
Notional principal: US$50 million

Adjustment of notional principal: In the event that any of the issuers makes an early repayment in respect of a underlying credit asset, the notional principal will be reset on the next payment date to reflect the outstanding value of the remaining loans.

Maturity: five years from commencement date
Commencement date: ten business days

Payments: Dealer pays enhanced payments, investor pays interest payments.
Enhanced payments: three month Libor plus 0.25% paid quarterly on an actual/360 basis
Interest payments: three month Libor paid quarterly on an actual/360 basis

Underlying credit assets:	*Issuer*	*Maturity*
	Country A	December 2000
	Country B	June 1999
	Country C	April 2000
	Country D	December 2000

Average coupon: Libor plus[20]bps pa

Event of default: If any one of the issuers files for bankruptcy protection or incurs a payment default on any debt which remains unpaid for 5 business days, the swap will be terminated and the investor will pay the termination payment to the dealer who will pay to the investor the termination asset.

▶

▶ **Termination payment:** Equal to the notional principal
Termination asset: The defaulted underlying credit asset to the amount of face value equal to the notional principal.
Calculation agent: [Dealer]

Fig 2.3

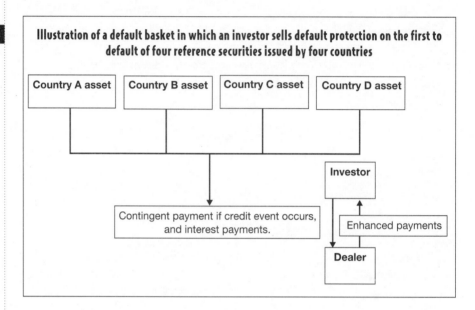

Illustration of a default basket in which an investor sells default protection on the first to default of four reference securities issued by four countries

Example

Achieving revenue neutral diversification by using a default substitution swap

Trade objective: Another common use of credit default swaps is to achieve revenue neutral diversification. Typically, the object is to reduce the risk of the credit portfolio without reducing expected returns by using credit swaps to achieve revenue neutral diversification.

Consider a bank with 20% of its total loan portfolio committed to European retail companies – a clear concentration of risk.

Further suppose the bank has no exposure to Latin mining companies, which are determined to have a low default correlation with its existing portfolio. This bank could improve its risk-reward profile by, in combination, buying a credit swap (buying credit protection) to hedge a portion of its European retail exposure and selling a credit swap (selling credit protection) on a Latin mining company in an amount that generates revenue equal to the cost of the European retail risk hedge.

Resulting effect: Buying the credit swap virtually eliminated the credit exposure on a $50 million loan to a specific European retail company.

However, by itself, this transaction reduces portfolio revenues by the amount of the premium ($250,000 per annum).

Risk/Return portfolio profile: Without a sophisticated risk analysis system, a portfolio manager cannot be certain that the hedging alone improves the risk/return profile of the portfolio, because while it clearly reduces risk, it also reduces return.

However, selling the credit swap on the Latin mining company increases return by an amount that offsets the risk reduction. Also, providing the credit risk of the Latin mining company position is not greater than the credit risk of the original European retail position before hedging, the risk of the revised portfolio will be less than the risk of the original portfolio.

European retail credit swap: buy protection
Notional: $50 million
Reference asset: Loan
Maturity: four years
Currency: US$

Asian mining credit swap: sell protection
Notional: $45.54 million
Reference asset: Loan
Maturity: four years
Currency: US$

The absolute credit risk of the Latin American mining company (as measured by criteria such as public debt rating) does not necessarily need to be identical to the absolute credit risk of the European retail company. Key to the above trade example is the fact that the revenue generated by the new position (the notional times the spread) is approxi-

> If the spread income on two positions is almost identical, the market is indicating that the risk of loss from the two positions is roughly identical, notwithstanding differences in notional amount, spread and/or credit rating.

Key point

mately equivalent to the amount paid for the European retail hedge. The credit spread is the fair market price for the potential credit exposure. However, revenue neutral diversification works best if the credits 'exchanged' are of approximately the same credit quality and trade at approximately equal spreads, as this limits the degree to which large differences in notional amounts might distort the distribution of risk in the portfolio.

Enhancing access to higher quality asset returns using credit default swaps

A credit derivative like a default swap will allow a lower credit quality bank to invest in higher quality assets. In the past, lower credit quality banks have been forced to invest in riskier, higher yielding assets. Credit default swaps are now allowing investors with higher funding costs to compete effectively for high quality assets.

Example

Maturity	'A' rated assets yield	Bank XYZ acquiring 'A' rated asset on cash basis yields
1 year	3 month Libor + 5bps	−ve carry (Libor + 5bps − Libor + 20bps = −15bps)
5 year	3 month Libor + 20bps	flat carry (Libor + 20bps − Libor + 20bps = 0)

Credit rating: Bank XYZ rated BBB
Term funding: for Bank XYZ, three month Libor + 20bps
Objective: Bank XYZ would like to upgrade the credit quality of its portfolio by investing in 'A' rated assets.

Credit default swap sale: Bank XYZ sells five year protection on a five year 'A' rated asset to Counterparty ABC
Premium received: Bank XYZ receives 10bps per year
Premium paid: Counterparty ABC pays 10bps per year

Trade result: Given that the five year asset yields 20bps (flat carry for the bank), the credit swap provides a 10bps advantage over the cash transaction. (See Chapter 8.)

2 Total return swaps

In a total return swap trade, one counterparty pays the total return of an asset, including any interest payments and capital appreciation, in return for receiving a regular floating rate payment, such as Libor + spread. The total return payer effectively strips out all the economic exposure and credit risk to the underlying asset without having to sell it at the open market. The total return receiver gets exposure to the underlying asset at a financing rate which may be much lower than the rate at which it can raise funds in the market (especially if the receiver's credit rating is not so high).

Fig 2.4

Total return swap

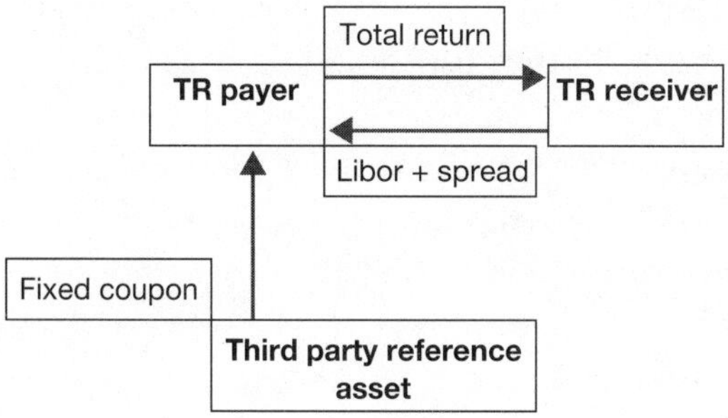

Total return

TR payer → TR receiver

Libor + spread

Fixed coupon

Third party reference asset

Note that in a total return swap there is no credit event and no contingent payment: at the end of each period, payments are automatically exchanged. In the event of default by the reference credit, the payment due at the end of the next period is brought forward to the time of default, the total return payment is determined by the dealer poll of the now defaulted asset, and the contract is terminated.

> *Note that in a total return swap there is no credit event and no contingent payment.*

The total return payer has hedged economic risk of an asset that it holds on balance sheet; the total return receiver is exposed to that risk but does not have any of the balance sheet, funding and operational complications of owning the asset. Typically, the spread paid by the total return payer would be competitive with its market borrowing spread.

Total return payers

Total return payers are typically lenders and investors who want to reduce or eliminate their exposure to an asset without removing it from their balance sheet or who want to finance a counterparty's synthetic acquisition of an asset. By keeping the asset on their books, they may avoid jeopardizing relationships with borrowers and breaching client confidentiality (since loan documentation and financial records are not transferred under a swap while they are under an outright sale). Total return payers, however, do not have to hold the asset on their balance sheets in order to pay the total return; if they do not, total return swaps can be an efficient way to short an asset synthetically.

Total return receivers

Total return receivers are typically insurance companies, hedge funds, corporate treasurers and other investors who want to put their cash to work on a leveraged basis, to diversify their portfolios or to achieve higher yields by taking on risk exposure. Risk management is often an integral part of their normal business. For example, some nonbank investors seek exposure to bank loans because they provide higher returns than bonds, relative to the risk. Total return swaps in effect allow them to make synthetic loans without the cost and administrative burden normally associated with lending.

Total return receivers lock in term financing rates and effectively create repurchase agreements in markets where repos may not exist. They can maximize the use of available capital by gaining exposure to an asset without buying it. They also avoid clearing, financing and execution associated with outright purchase. For certain types of institutions with capital constraints, total return swaps can provide the most economic way of using leverage to maximize their return on capital. Certain investment banks can structure, execute and hedge such transactions at a significantly lower cost than if an investor acquired and financed the transaction independently in the cash market.

Maturities

In practice, maturities on total return swaps rarely match the underlying asset. The swaps are shorter than the reference asset.

The total return payer negotiates a protection line for a limited amount of time without having to liquidate the asset. The receiver finances short and invests long.

Suppose a total return receiver wants six months' exposure to Eurotunnel, a distressed debt. What kind of conventional trades can satisfy this objective?

- buy a Eurotunnel ten year loan and sell in six months; or
- buy a six month call option on the ten year bond and sell a six month put option on the underlying ten year bond; or
- do a total return swap instead of the above trades.

In this case, it's a distressed debt so no interest payments and no fees apply. Only capital appreciation.

So if, for example, a total receiver finances for, say, two years (the duration of a particular swap), he may receive a total return tied to the performance of a ten year bond. It is much harder to estimate the probability of default for longer horizons.

Investor objectives: An investor desires exposure to a ten year BBB-corporate bond. The investor enters into a six month total return swap to finance the transaction.

Example

Assumption:

Asset:	$100MM face value 7.5% BBB-corporate
Trade date:	4 October 1999
Maturity:	10 October 1999
Total return payer:	Bank XYZ
Total return receiver/	
Floating rate payer:	Investor ABC
Six month Libor setting:	5.5%
Financing spread:	25bps
Term of swap:	six months

At inception:

All in bond price/notional	
amount:	102

At termination:	Scenario 1	Scenario 2
All in bond price:	*104 3/8*	*100*
Coupon:	$3,750,000	$3,750,000
Capital gain/(loss):	$2,375,000	$(2,000,000)
Investor receives:	$6,125,000	$1,750,000
Interest period:	182 days (182/360)	182 days (182/360)
Floating payment:	$2,906,944	$2,906,944
Net cash flow:	$3,218,056	–$1,156,944

At termination, the bond would be valued according to the prevailing market price based on a dealer poll. The investors may be given an opportunity to participate in the poll.

Some investment applications for total return swaps

Synthetic high yield debt trading

I will now look at some typical uses of total return swaps. Synthetic high yield debt trading is simply obtaining exposure to a bank loan via a total return swap. Capital structure arbitrage is where a perceived mispricing between bank loans and sub-debt of the same issue is exploited. Diversifying concentrated exposures in a portfolio can also be achieved using total return swaps. Finally, the most common use by banks is the freeing up of credit limits.

Investor objective: Let's assume an investor seeks to attain $10 million of exposure to an outstanding bank loan or a loan syndication.

Problems: However, this investor has limited access to the cash loan market, limited back office capabilities, and relatively high funding costs.

Solution: The investor can use a total return swap to gain exposure to the bank loan while keeping it off the balance sheet.

Leverage investment: The investor can choose to leverage its investment by holding in reserve, or pledging to the total return swap counterparty, i.e. a major investment bank, $1 million against the $10 million underlying exposure. Further assume that the underlying loan related swap payment to the investor is Libor + 2.50%, while the payment to the investment bank counterparty is Libor + 1.00%. The 150 basis points spread is leveraged ten times to 15.0% in respect to the investor's $1 million investment. Add to this the yield on the $1 million of, say, 6.0%, and the swap generates a current annual yield of 21.0%.

Downside: Of course leverage works both ways, a default on the loan (reference asset) and a subsequent recovery of even as much as 90% of the $10 million loan will still result in the investor suffering a 100% loss, i.e. all of his $1 million pledge to the investment bank counterparty he did the total return swap with (10% loss of $10 million is $1 million).

Summary of trade

Asset:	$10 million of exposure to an outstanding bank loan
Trade date:	4 October 1999
Maturity:	10 October 1999
Total return payer:	Bank XYZ
Total return receiver/ Floating rate payer:	Investor ABC receives Libor + 250bps and pays Libor + 100bps
Financing spread:	150bps
Term of swap:	six months
Amount pledged:	Investor ABC pledged $1 million to Bank XYZ
Yield on pledged amount:	6% of $1 million
Total yield on pledged amount:	(150bps × 10) + 6% = 15% + 6% = 21%

Capital structure arbitrage

Investor objective: Investors can also use total return swaps to arbitrage a perceived mispricing between bank loans and subordinate debt of the same issuer.

Arbitrage opportunity: For example, suppose that both assets are priced at par, but the loan yields Libor + 375 basis points while the debt yields (on swapped basis) Libor + 275 basis points. Clearly, in the absence of some overriding technical or other non-market factors, a mispricing exists since the senior, secured asset yields more than the subordinated asset.

Solution: To efficiently exploit this opportunity, a total return swap can be executed to effectively go long the bank loan and short the subordinated debt at a ratio of, say, two to one (synthetically long $20 million bank loan and short $10 million subordinate debt). In one total return swap we receive the bank loan total return and pay some kind of floating rate payment, in the other total return swap we pay a total on the subordinate debt and receive some kind of floating payment.

Assumptions: If we assume the investor pays Libor + 275 basis points on $10 million and Libor + 125 basis points on another $10 million.

Initial investment and resulting yield: This structure generates a positive carry of 175 basis points [(100bps*$10/$20) + (250bps*$10/$20)] on $20 million. Assuming a $2 million cash investment, this spread is leveraged ten times into a 17.5% return. Add this to the 6.0% cash return, and the structure generates a yield of 23.5% per annum.

Diversifying concentrated portfolios

Objective: Many institutions face a problem known as the 'credit paradox'. Limited credit-origination resources and the need to specialize in order to maximize efficiency inherently result in a concentrated credit exposure for such institutions. However, a diversified portfolio is required in order to achieve an optimal risk/return profile. Traditional cash market mechanisms fail to fully address the problem for a variety of reasons, including:

- relationship maintenance
- the lack of broad distribution capabilities
- underlying market liquidity.

To solve the 'credit paradox', the user can enter into a total return swap to diversify its risk without actually selling the underlying loans, thereby maintaining good client relations while pushing out towards the efficient frontier. ▶

▶

Freeing up credit lines

Objectives: Assume a commercial bank has reached its internal credit limits to borrowers, trading partners or traditional derivatives counterparties. Assume a commercial bank has reached its internal lending limits with respect to a certain client, but must continue to provide for the upcoming funding needs or derivative transactions of the client in order to maintain a strong relationship.

Solution: To address this problem, the bank enters into a total return swap with an investment bank dealing in credit derivatives, tied to an underlying loan(s). Under the swap, the bank pays the total return on the existing loan position(s) in consideration for a Libor-based payment.

Result: The reference asset(s) stays on the books, the bank has effectively swapped the borrower's or the derivative counterparty's credit risk for that of the investment bank counterparty, thereby freeing up corresponding credit lines.

Repurchase agreement (repo) versus a total return (TR) swap

Before attempting to compare repos with total return swaps, it is helpful to look at repos in a little more detail.

A classic repo

Repos are repurchase agreements.

Definition

> A **repo** is an agreement to buy(sell) a security while at the same time agreeing to sell(buy) the same security at a predetermined future date. The price at which the reverse transaction takes place sets the interest rate over the period (the repo rate).

The most active repo market is the US, where the federal reserve sets short-term interest rates by lending securities. In a reverse repo the buyer sells cash in exchange for a security. Repos can benefit both parties. Buyers of repos often receive a better return than that available on equivalent money market instruments; and financial institutions, particularly dealers, are able to get sub-Libor funding. A variation on the repo is the buy/sell back. The buy/sell back's coupon becomes the property of the purchaser for the duration of the agreement. It is preferred by credit sensitive investors such as central banks.

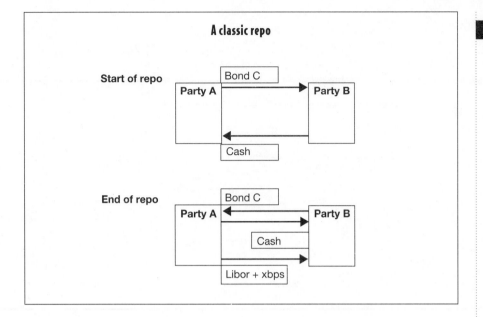

A classic repo

Fig 2.5

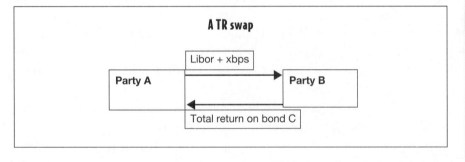

A TR swap

Fig 2.6

Figure 2.5 is a classic repo and Figure 2.6 shows a TR swap. Party B is hedging its market and credit risk by laying it off to party A. Party A wants the exposure to bond C. The alternative is for party A to purchase bond C, but this involves financing costs. Via the swap, party A may achieve lower financing cost than it would normally pay to finance the bond. The TR swap is like a financed purchase of a bond, similar to a repo.

A TR swap combined with the sale of a bond

Say that party A already owns bond C and wants to finance it. Party A sells the bond to party B and simultaneously enters into a TR swap with party B (see Figure 2.7). If party A were to repo the bond to party B, and if the repo rate was Libor + xbps, the TR swap + the bond sale would mimic the repo transaction.

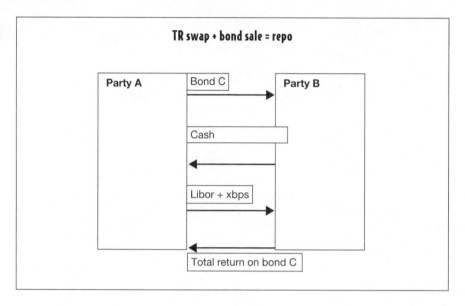

Fig 2.7

TR swap + bond sale = repo

There are clear similarities between the TR swap and the repo, a fact that has not escaped repo traders. Many repo traders use the TR swap since it may offer a more economical financing rate and also allows them to remove the bond from their balance sheets for the duration of the swap.

The credit derivative market and the repo market are linked by the shared use of the structure. It is billed as a credit derivative but has other uses, including the financing function typically achieved by a repo or a sale/buy back.

A dealer who wants to finance an asset for a short time (say overnight) can do so in the repo market, especially if the asset is a US treasury security. Even a dealer who wants to finance for a longer time, say a year, can do so in the repo market. However, longer-term deals and esoteric assets may require funding through the TR swap.

The credit derivative structure may be a more efficient means of achieving the same objective: a financed position. You receive the cash that you need plus all the upside (or downside) of the bond.

Consider a dealer with a view that bond C (which he does not own) is going to fall in price:

■ **He can go short the bond and borrow it in the repo market**
  In this case, he pays away the risk on bond C and receives a Libor spread on the proceeds of the short sale. The dealer is short the bond, which (for example) yields 10 per cent. If the bond is special (see

Chapter 8), he will earn Libor minus 100bps on his cash.

If Libor is 6 per cent the dealer losses 500bps, annually.

■ **Alternatively, the dealer could go into a TR swap in which he agrees to pay the TR on bond C.**

The dealer, B, is hoping that the price of the bond will decline by more than the negative carry. If the breakeven is better using TR swap, then the TR swap will be used as opposed to a repo.

In cases involving specials, where the reverse repo rate is quite low and therefore the implied financing cost is high, the TR swap may make a lot more sense.

Balance sheet considerations

The TR swap has the capacity to remove the bond position from the balance sheet. One method banks use to avoid internal and external reporting requirements, is to balloon up the balance sheet inter-month and inter-quarter. Then a TR swap can be used to get everything pared down for month-end and quarter-end reporting and for window dressing. They will do a one week TR swap right over the reporting date.

The reason that the bonds go off the balance sheet in a sale plus TR swap is that they are sold outright. A repo involves a commitment to buy the bonds back so they are *not* removed from the balance sheet. A sale plus a TR swap includes no such obligation. The counterparty is not required to sell the bonds back to the original owner or even to sell the bonds at all. Presumably a firm will use classic repos intra-month and total return swaps when possible over the reporting periods.

Balance sheet uses ('synthetic repo'), summary

A growing use of TROR swaps as synthetic repo is another application for the total rate of return swap. There is now a new sector of the investment community that has the analytic skills to buy the credit but does not want the funded instrument.

This kind of firm collateralizes TROR with hedge funds. Note that this use of credit derivatives to split the funded instrument from the risk has an exact parallel with interest rate swaps. Interest rate swaps liberated the trading of interest rate risk from the taking and placing of deposits or the purchase and sale of bonds; credit derivatives likewise allow a wider range of participants to trade credit risk. At the same time, since the motivation of the hedge funds will usually be different from the traditional lending bank relationship, there are potential problems here, which we return to in Chapter 7.

Another use of TROR swaps has been to manage balance sheets. One technique has been the use of total rate of return swaps to create short-term funding vehicles.

Assume an investment bank creates a trust to which is transferred $2.5 billion of investment grade bonds. It would appear likely that the legal costs of creating such a trust, if the trust is one of a series which is being repeatedly created and then dissolved so that the legal documentation becomes standardized, might be of the order of, say, $50,000. Similarly, it is likely that the rating agencies, if called upon to rate such trusts repeatedly during the course of a year, might be persuaded to reduce the standard rating fees. Let us suppose that the cost of arranging a rating for such an entity is also $50,000. Broadly speaking, therefore, the aggregate costs of setting up such a trust might be, say, $100,000. Supposing that the aggregate amount of the trust is $2.5 billion, then for a two month period, if we can achieve a saving of 3bps on our funding, we will save (neglecting day-count considerations) the sum of $125,000. Thus the operation becomes worthwhile if we can save 3bps on our funding costs. This is by no means possible if we bear in mind that the trust as a separate entity might well be attractive to some investors with large exposures to investment banks.

In the above example, the trust will have a short lived, defined life. It will not be engaged in any of the speculative trading typical of some investment banks. If the underlying securities are Treasury bonds, it would probably not be difficult for the trust to achieve quite a good rating, even in the presence of a total rate of return swap between the trust and investment bank to pass the market value of the position back to the investment bank.

A quite separate use of such structures is also fairly well known in the marketplace, namely the use of these trusts by Japanese entities to 'park' assets in them over balance sheet dates. Such 'window dressing', to be effective, does require generous accounting treatment and therefore is probably of less use to entities from a number of other countries.

The Japanese have started to inspect much more closely US and European banks that help Japanese firms in 'window dressing' their losses. To be balanced, Japanese institutions should also be inspected, although none of these Japanese, US or European entities has broken the law.

Selling credit risk

Repo teams, just like any other lenders of money accumulate credit exposures. They may use some credit derivatives to lay off some of that exposure. Typically the pressure to do a credit derivative or default swap comes from the internal risk management department, which may have a sour view on country exposure: for instance, Asia's recent stock market decline influences and total country exposures. So select country credit need to be reduced. A credit default swap or a credit linked note may also be used for that purpose.

What is a credit derivative?

There is considerable uncertainty in the market about when an instrument is a credit derivative and when it is not. One definition of a CD is any contract whose economic performance is primarily linked to the credit performance of the underlying asset. This definition would technically rule out TR swaps as their performance is only partly linked to the credit quality of the underlying asset and mostly linked to the market risk of the underlying asset.

MGM Grand – total return swap (as of 20 October 1997)

Example

Underlying index: MGM Grand Hotels Finance 12% due 1 May 2002 (B1/BB-)

Current price: 109.50 (Treasury 5/97+2.70%)

Notional principal amount: $10.95 million ($10 million face value of the underlying index)

Settlement date: One week
Maturity date: 5 May 2000
Total payer: Bank
Total return payments: The bank pays all coupon and principal repayments to the investor two days after they are received.

Fixed rate payer: The investor
Fixed rate payment dates: Quarterly
Fixed rate: 8.50% (or three months Libor + 1.25%), Act/360 paid on notional principal amount.

Collateral required: $2,190,000 which is 20% of market value of the debt, in cash or US Government securities. This transaction will be marked to market and the collateral adjusted on a weekly basis.

Settlement: On the maturity date the investor will have the option to: (a) take delivery of the underlying debt plus any cash or securities repaid, in exchange for $10.95 million plus the fixed rate payment; or (b) cash settle the transaction at the then prevailing market rates.

▶

► **Summary**

In this transaction, the investor receives a leveraged return on the MGM Grand Hotels 12% First Mortgage bonds due 1 May 2002 and pays a fixed rate.

If no default occurs, the investor pays 8.50%*10.95 = $930,750 every year.

The investor receives 12.00%*10 = $1,200,000 every year.

Net amount received by investor = $1,200,000 – $930,750 = $269,250, if we assume a risk free rate of 5% return on the collateral, plus above return. The total return on the collateral 12.29% + 5% = 17.29%.

3 Credit options

Before discussing credit options, it is important to note some general characteristics of credit spread derivatives and credit spreads.

Key point

> Credit spreads represent the margin relative to the risk free rate designed to compensate the investor for the risk of default on the underlying security.

The credit spread itself is calculated as:

Credit spread = Yield of security or loan minus yield of corresponding risk free security

Two general formats of credit spread derivatives exist:

- credit spreads relative to the risk free benchmark (the absolute spread)
- credit spreads between two credit sensitive assets (the relative spread).

The central concept of credit spread oriented credit derivatives is the isolation and capture of value as a result of:

- relative credit value changes independent of changes in interest rates
- trading forward credit spread expectation
- trading the term structure of credit spread.

The central concept underlying credit spread products is the ability to use credit spread derivatives to trade, hedge or monetize expectations on future credit spreads.

(I will concentrate in this section on non linear (option) types of investment. There are also linear (forward) types of investment.)

> **Credit options** are derivative instruments with payoffs linked to the credit characteristics of a particular underlying asset or issuer.

Many asset managers have portfolios that are sensitive to changes in the spread between riskless and risky assets, and credit derivatives are an efficient way to manage this exposure. There may be several reasons a seller of credit protection may be willing to assume the credit risk of an underlying financial asset. For instance, a high-yield manager may wish to increase his overall exposure to the risky debt market, or he may want to target specific

Credit derivatives represent a natural extension of the financial markets' capacity to unbundle risk.

credit risks to enhance a portfolio's income. Conversely, the buyer of the credit derivative transfers the credit exposure, but not the asset itself, to the derivative seller. This allows a financial institution, such as a bank or an insurance company, to maintain economic exposure to high-yielding assets, but without the risk of downgrades.

Credit derivatives represent a natural extension of the financial markets' capacity to unbundle risk. They offer an important method for asset managers to hedge their exposure to credit risk, because they permit the transfer of the exposure from one party to another. But the two main types of credit options – those triggered by a decline in value of an asset and those triggered by a change in the asset's spread over the risk free rate – follow distinctly different stochastic processes, and the differences have important implications for how the derivatives are priced within a contingent claims format.

I will call the two primary types of credit options Type 1 and Type 2. The first type is a **put** where the option writer agrees to compensate the option buyer for a decline in value of the financial asset below the strike price. In practice, Type I credit options are usually specified in terms of the acceptable default spread of a bond. That is, upon exercise of the credit option, the payoff is determined by subtracting the market price of the bond from the strike price, where the strike price is determined by taking the present value of the bond's cash flow discounted at the risk free rate plus the strike credit spread.

Type 1 credit options are compound options because risky debt itself is valued as the difference between a riskless bond and a put option on firm value. That is, risky debt holders have effectively sold a put option to the equity holders of the firm. Should the value of the firm's assets decline below the face value of its outstanding debt, equity holders may put the firm's assets back to the debt holders and walk away from the firm.

Type 2 credit options are specified as **call** options on the level of the credit spread. This type of option is structured so that the option is in-the-money when the credit spread exceeds the specified (strike) spread level. The payoff is the difference in the credit spread times a specified notional value.

Investor use of credit spread options

FM

For example, an investor might sell an option to bank A, for which the investor is paid an up-front premium. The option gives bank A the right to sell a bond to the investor at a certain strike price expressed in terms of a spread over a benchmark. On the option's exercise date, if the actual spread of the underlying bond is lower than the strike price, the option expires worthless and the investor pays nothing. If it is higher, bank A delivers the bond and the investor pays a price whose yield spread over the benchmark equals the strike spread.

In this case, the investor may simply want to generate premium income in order to increase the current yield on its portfolio. On the other hand, it may be taking a position on the spread level at which the bond becomes a bargain. If the option expires worthless, the investor acquires the bond at a spread level that it considered attractive. Indeed, after taking the premium income into account, investors can sometimes purchase bonds in this way on quite favourable terms, compared with current prices.

Investors can also use options on credit spreads to make a position on the relative performance of two different bonds, without actually buying or selling either one, again stripping out interest rate risk to focus on pure credit risk. For example, an investor might take the view that Brazil's external US dollar bonds will outperform Argentina's external US dollar bonds over the next year, reflecting a greater improvement in Brazil's credit risk. By structuring a transaction using options on the two countries' sovereign dollar bonds, with bank A as the counterparty, the investor could profit if, after a year, Brazil had tightened more or widened less than Argentina, resulting in a tighter relative spread. Such transactions are typically off balance sheet and exploit the power of leverage.

In another variation on the basic structure, investors can sell puts and buy calls to lock in a current spread, possibly earning premium income in the process. This can allow an investor to buy one or more underlying bonds in a capital-efficient way, using the leverage of options to establish a synthetic position rather than buying the bonds in the cash market.

Credit put options

Credit put options are quoted:

- on the price of a bond – **price options** – used mostly for floating rate notes; or
- on the spread between the bond's yield to maturity and the yield to maturity of the corresponding treasury **spread options** – used mostly for fixed rate notes.

The buyer of the put is entitled to put a specific bond to the seller at a predetermined spread. The seller of the put receives an up-front premium.

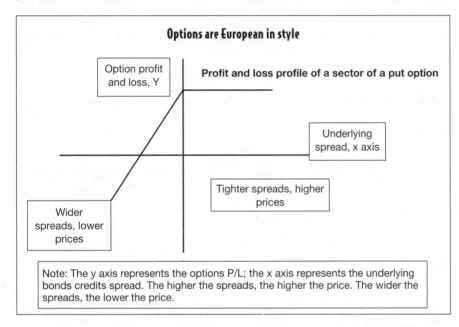

Options are European in style

Option profit and loss, Y

Profit and loss profile of a sector of a put option

Underlying spread, x axis

Tighter spreads, higher prices

Wider spreads, lower prices

Note: The y axis represents the options P/L; the x axis represents the underlying bonds credits spread. The higher the spreads, the higher the price. The wider the spreads, the lower the price.

Fig 2.8

Let's summarize the reasons why an investor would sell a credit put option. By selling a credit put, the investor monetizes his view about the level at which a given bond is a good buy:

Possible scenarios

- if the option expires worthless, the option seller pockets the premium;
- if the option holder exercises the option, the option seller purchases the bond at a level which has been determined in advance to be a good buy. The option seller still gets to keep the premium;
- after adjusting for the premium received, the option seller's break-even purchase price for the bond is very often favourable compared to today's price.

Let's also look at an application summary of credit spread options and a simple put credit spread option example.

- profiting from a spread tightening;
- increase the current yield of a portfolio, particularly one which may be overweighted in cash;
- receive premium income for purchasing bonds in the future at a level which seems attractive.

Credit spread options allow an investor to profit from a spread view. They also increase the current yield of the portfolio, particularly one that may be overweight in cash (i.e. the portfolio being overweight in the most risky instrument must have the least yield). The most obvious benefit is that the investor receives premium income for purchasing bonds in the future.

The most typical use of credit put options is to sell a basket of put options against a portfolio of bonds. Another is to sell the underlying cash bond today and also sell a put option. Set the strike of the put at a level where you will be happy to purchase the bond back.

Example

Put credit spread on ABC bonds due 31 December 2023 (as of 14 November 1998)

Spread put buyer: Bank
Spread put seller: Investor
Notional principal amount: $10 million
Settlement date: Today
Exercise date: One year from today
Underlying index: ABC bonds due 31 December 2023
Reference US Treasury: The offer yield of the US Treasury 6.25% due August 2023.
Index credit spread: The yield to maturity of the underlying index using the flat bid price (bid price net of accrued interest and any non-paid coupons) of the underlying index minus the offer yield of the reference US Treasury at 12.00 pm New York E.S.T. time two days before exercise date.
Current spread: 1.95%
Spread put strike: 2.05% (at the money forward strike)
Put option payment: Notional * max (DUR*(Index credit spread – 2.05%),0)
DUR (duration): Eight
Option premium: 1.25% of the notional principal amount payable by the bank to the investor on the settlement date.

Looking at the above term sheet, note the 'interesting' use of bid and offer prices. When the offer price is high, the offer yield is low, when the bid price is low, the bid yield is high. When we subtract (the bid yield of the underlying index – the offer yield of the reference US treasury), we increase the expected value of the index credit spread.

How credit spread options are quoted

Table 2.3 shows the traditional format for a range of indicative quotations on premiums for options on the bond credit spreads for a hypothetical range of securities.

Table 2.3 Indicative pricing of bond credit spread options

Type of option	European call options on the spread at the strike spread	European call options on the spread at the strike spread	European call options on the spread at the strike spread
Issuer	A Corporation	B Corporation	C Corporation
Rating	Baa3/BBB–	A2/A	Baa2/BBB
Underlying bond issue	8.000% 15 July 2023	6.875% 15 January 2003	8.625% 15 April 2020
Reference Treasury	6.25% August 2023	6.25% February 2023	6.25% August 2023
Spot spread (bps)	180	80	160
Strike spread (bps)	150	70	140
Premium (bps)	28	6	10
Type of option	**European put options on the spread at the strike spread**	**European put options on the spread at the strike spread**	**European put options on the spread at the strike spread**
Issuer	A Corporation	B Corporation	C Corporation
Rating	Baa3/BBB–	A2/A	Baa2/BBB
Underlying bond issue	8.000% 15 July 2023	6.875% 15 January 2003	8.625% 15 April 2020
Reference Treasury	6.25% August 2023	6.25% February 2023	6.25% August 2023
Spot spread (bps)	180	80	160
Strike spread (bps)	220	95	180
Premium (bps)	35	15	40

Summary

Table 2.4 A comparison of credit derivatives

Total return swap	Default swap	Secured loan trust note
Contractual agreement to exchange disparate cash flows, typically tied to asset's return and Libor	Contractual agreement to exchange fee for payment if a specified 'credit event' occurs	Debt or loan obligation with coupon and redemption tied to bank loan performance
Unlimited leverage	Unlimited leverage	Leverage up to ten times, seven for investment grade
Synthetic asset	Synthetic asset	Synthetic asset
Unlimited upside and downside	Fee limits buyer's downside and seller's upside. Seller has unlimited downside	Unlimited upside but limited downside (no margin calls)
Unrated	Unrated	Possibly investment grade
No exchange of principal	No exchange of principal	Principal changes hands
No voting rights	No voting rights	Limited voting rights
Off balance sheet	Off balance sheet	On balance sheet
No legal change of underlying asset ownership	No legal change of underlying asset ownership	No legal change of underlying asset ownership

We conclude this chapter by reviewing some of the key issues which arise in respect of credit derivatives.

Definition of a credit event

When dealing with a credit default swap or option it is important to define those 'credit events' which trigger a valuation of the reference credit and a payment by one of the parties. Some deals provide for only two credit events: a payment default on a reference credit or an insolvency of the reference credit. While these credit events are fairly easy to verify, other transactions use a list of a half dozen or more credit events. These range from credit rating upgrade or downgrade to a default by the same obligor on a different credit ('cross-default') or a restructuring of agreements relating to the reference credit. Some swaps provide for payouts if the credit spread over treasuries changes. This broader set of events may give more protection to the buyer of credit protection, but their occurrences may be hard to confirm. The description of the events in the agreement is often vague. It may need subjective judgement when dealing with, for example, 'material adverse effect'. Or delayed coupon payment by 24 hours – is that a default credit event?

Establishing that the credit event occurred

Credit derivative documents sometimes set out what is needed to prove a credit event has occurred. If an agreement includes a list of credit events that go beyond payment default and bankruptcy, it may be hard to produce clear evidence of a credit event. The agreement may have a materiality threshold. Or it may say that the credit event must be confirmed by third-party evidence such as publication of information about the default in a recognized source. This can lead to disputes if the agreed third-party source does not publish the information or if there is a delay in publication while the credit status of a reference continues to decline.

Rights to the reference credit

Some credit derivatives specify the rights of the parties regarding the reference credit. For example, a credit derivative (particularly forwards and some type of options) may provide for physical settlement through delivery of the reference credit. In some trades, the part holding the reference credit in its portfolio may agree not to accept certain changes to the reference asset without the counterpartys consent. However, it is more common for the agreement to leave the owner of the reference credit free to sell it, exercise its voting rights or take other actions, giving the counterparty no control rights over the reference credit.

Sharing information on the credit

If one party to a credit derivative holds the underlying reference credit, it may receive confidential information from the borrower (or from the agent for the syndicate or the trustee for security holders). There may be strong reasons for it not to disclose this information to the derivative counterparty. These might include confidentiality obligations under the credit agreement or securities laws. There might be a concern that premature disclosure could make it hard to restructure the credit. Hence it may be best, from the party's viewpoint, not to include in the credit derivative documentation any obligation to transmit information it receives, and to limit the credit events to those which have been publicly announced. On the other hand, from the viewpoint of the party taking the risk in the derivative, such information is clearly material. The question of insider trading may become relevant.

Credit Derivative Applications

Basic credit derivative trading applications

Basic credit derivative trading applications

Credit derivatives are used as an alternative to cash market investments, as an effective risk management tool and an efficient means to arbitrage different prices across asset classes. Credit derivatives can strip away credit risk in a more efficient manner than had previously been possible. In this chapter we will look at some of the simplest and the more complex trading applications of such credit derivatives.

> Credit derivatives provide market participants with efficient, tailor-made access to credit sensitive asset markets.

Key point

A total return swap credit derivative trading application

The following examples highlight all the various uses that credit derivatives can be applied to. Some are more common than others.

Example

Credit derivative investor needs can be summarized as follows:
- high yield return potential
- efficient access to bank loan markets
- off balance sheet investments
- minimal back office administration requirements
- low capital requirements.

Credit derivative potential investors can be categorized as follows:
- commercial banks
- investment banks
- hedge funds
- money managers.

Structure: The investor seeks $100 million of exposure and 'chooses' a leverage factor of ten times. The investor holds or posts a collateral of $10 million, generating a 6.5% return.

Total return swap: The investor receives $100 million bank loan total return (all interest, fees and realized price changes), assuming a yield of Libor + 250 bps. The investor pays the bank Libor + 100bps (see Figure 3.1).

Results
- The swap generates a 21.5% yield = (6.5% cash yield on the collateral + [150bps swap spread * 10 times]).
- Investor taps into the bank's distribution network for bank loans.

- Confidential, off balance sheet agreement.
- Simple swap administration rather than complicated bank loan administration.
- Potentially reduced capital requirements.

Risks: The investor can potentially lose much more than the $10 million – if the bank loan defaults.

Fig 3.1

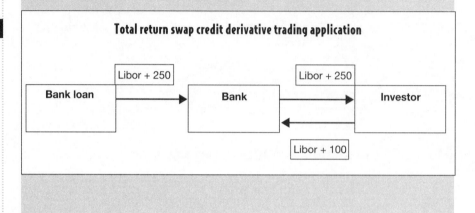

Total return swap credit derivative trading application

A secured loan trust note (SLT note) application

Example

Structure:
- The investor seeks $100 million of exposure and chooses a leverage of seven times.
- Investor purchases $14.3 million of SLT notes, issued by a trust.
- No margin calls.
- Trust receives $100 million bank loan portfolio proceeds (all interest, fees and realized price changes), assuming a yield of Libor + 250bps.
- Bank receives Libor + 100bps on $100 million (see Figure 3.2).

Results:
- Generates 17% expected yield (6.5% + 7*(150bps swap spread)).
- Investment grade rating BBB.
- Limited downside (the most the investor can lose is the $14.3 million).
- Simple note administration rather than complex loan administration.
- Investor taps into the bank's distribution network.
- Reduced capital requirements.

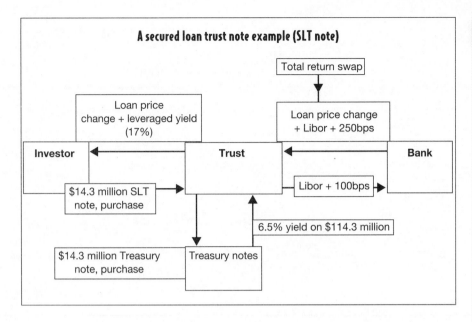

Fig 3.2

A secured loan trust note example (SLT note)

Risk management – total return swap applications

Credit derivative investor needs can be summed up as:
- diversified portfolio
- discretion.

Example

The 'credit paradox' does not allow the investor to achieve this in the cash market because:

- limited origination resources leads to specialization
- specialization leads to concentration
- concentration implies non-optimal portfolios.

Potential investors can be categorized as follows:
- commercial banks
- investment banks
- hedge funds
- money managers
- mutual funds
- pension funds.

Total return swap solution

Structure: A commercial bank (A) seeking diversification pays a large bank (B) the total return on $100 million concentrated loan portfolio.

The large bank (B) pays the commercial bank (A) the total return of a $100 million diversified loan portfolio (minus a spread). (See Figure 3.3.)

▶

Fig 3.3

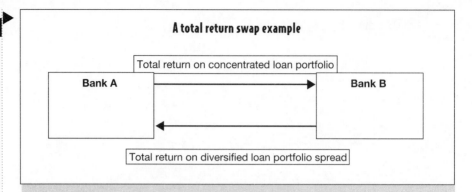

A total return swap example

- The commercial bank has effectively diversified its concentrated loan portfolio.
- The original loan remains on A's book to retain good client relationships.

Default swap solution

Investor needs are as follows:
- default protection
- discretion.

Potential investors can be categorized as follows:
- commercial banks
- investment banks
- hedge funds
- money managers
- mutual funds
- pension funds.

Structure: A commercial bank (A) pays a large bank (B) a quarterly fee. B pays A some stated amount if a specified 'credit event' occurs. Depending upon the structure, such credit related payments may involve A putting the underlying asset to B. (See Figure 3.4.)
- The commercial bank has effectively diversified its concentrated loan portfolio.
- The original loan remains on A's book to retain good client relationships.

Fig 3.4

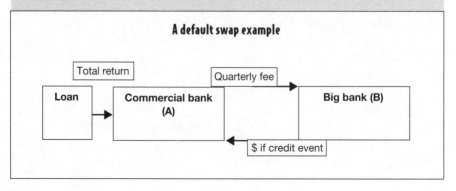

A default swap example

Credit Linked Notes

Introduction to credit linked notes (CLNs)

A credit linked note (CLN) enables an investor to purchase and fund an asset with a return linked to the credit risk of the asset itself and an additional credit risk transferred by way of a credit derivative between the issuer and the bank.

> A credit linked note structure enables the risks transferred using a credit swap to be embedded into a security and issued to an investor.

Key point

The investor receives a coupon and par redemption unless there has been a credit event by a reference credit, in which case redemption is equal to par minus a contingent payment. The transaction between the bank and the medium term note (MTN) issuer is a credit swap. The issuer receives a premium for taking exposure to the reference credit. This premium forms part of the coupon that is paid to the investor. Should there be a credit event by the reference credit, the issue redeems early, a contingent payment is made to the bank and the balance is paid to the investor.

There are two main risks assumed by the investor: that of the reference credit (by way of the credit default swap), and that of the MTN issuer. Should the reference credit default, this event would trigger an early and reduced redemption of the notes. Should the MTN issuer default, the investor is exposed to its recovery and to the mark to market of the credit swap at that time. This exposure to two risks is reflected in the yield on the note, which is the sum of the return of the MTN issuer and the premium of the credit swap.

Structured notes and credit linked notes

It is a simple matter to package a credit derivative inside a structured note. Typically, the investor receives a coupon and par redemption at maturity so long as there hasn't been a credit event.

Once a credit event occurs, the issuer calls the structure away from the investor and delivers the defaulting notes against them. Credit linked notes look very much like bonds and are, therefore, appealing to certain institutional investors which are prohibited from doing credit default swaps.

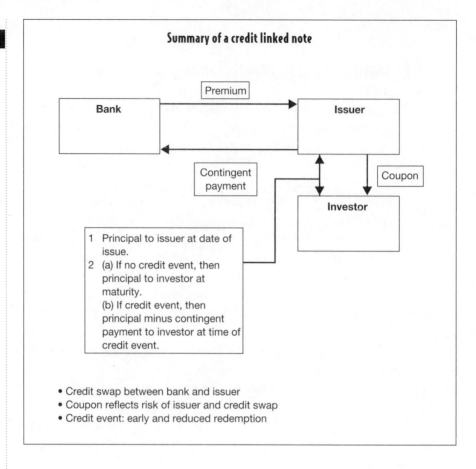

Fig 4.1

Summary of a credit linked note

Bank — Premium → Issuer

Contingent payment

Coupon

Investor

1. Principal to issuer at date of issue.
2. (a) If no credit event, then principal to investor at maturity.
   (b) If credit event, then principal minus contingent payment to investor at time of credit event.

- Credit swap between bank and issuer
- Coupon reflects risk of issuer and credit swap
- Credit event: early and reduced redemption

The issuer usually sets up a special purpose AAA rated vehicle. This vehicle sells default protection to a third counterparty in return for a premium. In return, the vehicle receives Xbps from the third counterparty. The investor purchases a structured note which pays a large coupon so long as no credit event happens.

Creation of structured notes

Before we look at some actual examples of credit linked notes, let's examine how structured products are created by banks to meet investor needs. There are three steps to creating structured notes, and we briefly look at each of these below:

- conceptual stage
- identification process
- structuring/construction stage.

Conceptual stage

The investor in the structured note/credit linked note has one of the following requirements:

- *View* – an investor has a certain view: interest rate, currency, commodity, volatility etc. and wishes to profit if these views come to pass.
- *Risk management* – investors may have risks that need to be hedged, but are prohibited from executing the required hedge by themselves.
- *Asset-liability management* – investors who have either a fixed or a contingent liability cash flow on specific dates may need to hedge themselves.
- *Arbitrage/timing* – market conditions may be at extreme levels which are rarely reached. A client may wish to profit if they return to their 'normal' levels.
- *Diversification/asset allocation* – these structures can provide exposures to different classes of investments: domestic and non-domestic fixed income markets, equity, currency and commodity markets etc.

Identification process

Once the idea has been conceptualized, the equivalent views that are necessary to the construction of the note can be distilled from these concepts. The general type of structure can then be selected based on these views and the components required for the assembly of the structure identified. This customization stage can be divided into five steps:

- *Nationality* – the first risk factor is the country in which the investor has a view. This will severely limit the scope of instruments available. Most of the time, investors express domestic views so the answer to the nationality question is the native country itself. At other times, investors want to express a view on a foreign market (e.g. an emerging market).
- *Rate profile* – the question as to what the investor's rate profile is like needs to be asked. Is the investor, for example, bullish on interest

rates? Or bearish? Also a distinction needs to be drawn between short-term rates and the yield curve in general. Is the view that short-term rates will remain low, or rise high, will the yield curve flatten or steepen? See Table 4.1, linking these rate profiles to the most aptly structured notes.

■ *Risk/Return* – the investor's risk return profile is crucial in determining the amount of risk embedded in the note. The risk tolerance for coupon and principal payments must be examined (see Table 4.2). Embedded within the risk/return profile is the investor's strategic view.

■ *Maturity and credit* – these provide the 'finishing touches' on the structure. The investor's maturity profile and credit appetite are taken into account (see Table 4.3). Almost 80 per cent of the structures have maturities shorter than three years. All are highly rated issuers. If an investor is taking a market risk, he typically prefers to avoid taking on relatively large credit risk. For longer time horizons, the credit rating of the issuer becomes more and more important.

Table 4.1 Rate profiles and the relevant structures that could be used

Interest rate and yield curve view	Economic view	Products to satisfy these views
Short rates: low. Yield curve: flatten	Low inflation expectation, slow economic growth	Floored FRN, indexed amortized notes, yield curve accrual note, inverse FRN
Short rates: low. Yield curve: steepen	Some inflation expectation, slow economic growth	CMT, capped/leveraged cap FRN
Short rates: rise high. Yield curve: flatten	Low to fair inflation expectation, strong economic growth	Libor FRN, accrual note based on CMT, superfloater based on Libor, Libor-CMS/CMT

Table 4.2 Investor's strategic view is embedded within the risk/return profile

Risk/Return	Coupon structure	Principal structure
Low	Minimum coupon > 0 Incremental yield pickup	No principal risk
Medium	Minimum coupon = 0 Medium yield increment	No principal risk
High	Minimum coupon = 0 Low to very high yield increment	Principal risk

Table 4.3 Maturity profile and credit profile appetite for investors

Maturity	Form	Issuer
Under 1 year	CP	A1/P1
1 to 3 years	CD, MTN, bank notes	Banks, corporations
More than 3 years	MTN, bond	US agencies

Risk/Return basic strategies

There are two basic risk/return strategies:

- *Trading* – a structure with high leverage, high risk/high return, may have principal risk. The time horizon is an intermediate date.
- *Buy and hold* – a structure with low leverage, enhanced coupon at low risk and no principal risk. The time horizon is to maturity.

In addition, the following characteristics of a buy and hold structure should be noted:

- *Low leverage* – the investor often wishes to obtain a steady level of return over the life of the note and thus prefers to avoid high leverage.
- *Enhanced cash flow* – the investor is willing to accept a low measure of risk to obtain an incremental yield enhancement. The enhancement can range from 5 to 200 basis points.
- *Minimum coupon protection* – the investor prefers a non zero coupon to protect himself if interest rates move in an adverse direction.
- *No redemption rate risk* – the investor wishes to obtain par at redemption to protect himself if interest rates move in an adverse direction.
- *Typical investors* – pension funds, banks, regionally based investors.

A smaller class of investors consider a trading strategy in structured notes. They require a structure that can gain value very quickly if rates move in the right direction. The trading horizon is usually short term. However the maturity of the note can be longer to provide greater leverage. These types of investors would like:

- high risk
- high potential returns
- redemption linked structures (they may like a 60–70 per cent floor). This is a lower floor than that which is required by buy and hold strategies.

Structuring or construction stage

Obtain the correct market price for each component. This stage requires the pricing of each component in a structure and then pricing the whole structure.

An example of a credit linked note

Towards the end of 1996, JP Morgan issued two credit linked notes worth more than $1 billion. The first of the two was issued in September 1996 – a $594 million ten year note tied to Walmart, the AA rated US retailer. Another deal of a similar size was done on 18 December 1996 on a second reference credit. The credit linked note market is one of the fastest growing areas in credit derivatives. The Walmart note was originally priced at 65bps over comparable US treasuries. It has tightened to 60bps. A comparable Walmart note trades at 40–45bps over treasuries. The extra premium is due to the exposure to the credit linked note, to trust and also to illiquidity concerns.

> It is easy to find clients willing to purchase the credit linked note. What is more difficult is to find counterparties for the other leg of the swap – someone willing to pay for credit protection.

JP Morgan does not reveal its motives for arranging the deal. It may have been approached by Wall Street banks wanting to reduce their exposure to Walmart. Or maybe Walmart has gone through a capital restructuring programme which required it to lay off some of the risk to its own subordinated debt.

Materiality clause

JP Morgan has written a materiality clause into the deal whereby Walmart spreads must widen to at least 150bps above the US Treasury in order for a credit event to be announced. The dealer also set up an elaborate discovery mechanism for the recovery value in case of default. JP Morgan will conduct a poll of five leading market makers every two weeks for three months to find the price of the defaulted debt.

In case of default, investors have an extra option:

- they can go for an early redemption based on a poll conducted immediately after default;
- they can wait for later redemption based on the true recovery value of Walmart's debt;
- if no such value becomes apparent, JP Morgan will conduct another poll after an 18 month cooling down period.

Why would a financial institution use CLNs?

The re-engineering of credit derivatives into a structured note format is motivated by the traditional factors which dictate the use of these structures generally. However, there are a number of additional factors which are also relevant, including:

- the capacity to participate in markets which traditionally have excluded participation from investors, such as the bank loan market;
- the ability to create exposure to particular markets where direct exposure is either prohibited, difficult or expensive as a result of either regulations or high transaction costs;
- the ability to assume exposure to credit risk where the performance obligation (i.e. the issuer) is separate, in a credit sense, from the underlying credit risk, allowing investment in assets or asset classes which traditionally have not been available;
- the capacity to create rated formats for investment in traditionally unrated assets;
- the ability to add credit risk as a unique and specified asset class or risk factor to investment portfolios.

This is in addition to the more conventional advantages of these structures such as customization of exposure and structured forms of tradeable risk.

Types of credit linked notes

Credit linked notes fall into two categories of transaction:

- *traditional forms of structured notes* – featuring a linkage of either coupon or principal to an underlying credit risk component issued by a high quality issuer where the issuer in turn hedges out its exposure fully with a back-to-back credit derivative transaction with a dealer.
- *synthetic bonds* – entailing the issue of debt where the underlying

credit risk exposure is created through a credit derivative transaction designed to replicate the characteristics of a fixed interest security issued by the underlying issuer. These transactions are typically similar to asset repackaging transactions utilizing credit derivatives.

Total rate of return credit linked notes

The main objective of total rate of return credit linked notes is the simulation of an investment in the underlying loan asset (bank loan or bond) or an index based on a basket of the underlying loan assets.

The structure of TRR CLNs

The structure allows a separation of the risk profiles with direct credit risk on the issuer and the underlying market risk exposure to the high yield issuers underlying the index.

Example

Total return loan swap index note

Issuer: AAA/AA rated institution

Principal amount: US$50 million

Maturity (years): The earlier of: (a) One year from commencement date. (b) The next succeeding payment date following default on the underlying credit asset.

Underlying credit asset: Loan to [XYZ Corporation] dated [15 March 1995]

Coupon: Three month Libor plus margin payable quarterly on an actual/360 day basis.

Margin: [250] bps pa

Principal redemption: At par plus capital price adjustment subject to the minimum redemption level.

Minimum redemption level: 0%

Capital price adjustment: Principal amount times change (either positive or negative) in the price of the underlying credit asset. The price of the underlying credit asset is calculated as (current price – initial price)/initial price.

Initial loan price: 100 or face value

Current loan price: The [bid or offer] price of the underlying index as calculated by the calculation agent in accordance with the calculation method at 11.00 am (New York Time) two business days prior to each payment date.

Calculation method:

- in the sole opinion of the calculation agent; or
- by dealer poll under which the calculation agent will poll at least four and no more than six dealers in the loan and utilize the quoted prices to determine an average price for the loan; or
- by reference to a screen or quote service.

Calculation agent: [Dealer]

The above structure can be decomposed into two separate transactions which are combined:

- an investment by the investor in a floating rate asset such as a Libor based FRN; and
- the simultaneous entry by the investor into a total return swap where the investor pays the floating interest rate index (Libor) and receives the total return on the underlying loan asset.

The issuer will, in this case, enter into the total return swap to eliminate any exposure to fluctuations in the index and to allow generation of a known cost of funds (consistent with its funding cost objectives).

Figures 4.2 and 4.3 below show the construction of such a trade.

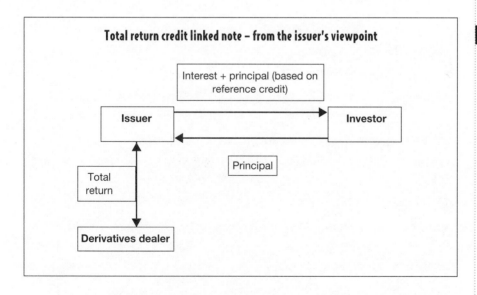

Total return credit linked note – from the issuer's viewpoint

Fig 4.2

Fig 4.3

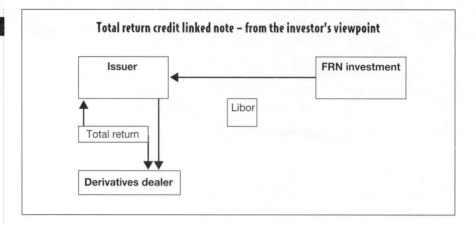

Total return credit linked note – from the investor's viewpoint

Two aspects of this type of note merit comment: the ability to introduce leverage; and the capacity to effectively short sell the relevant loan or bond market to capture value from a decline in the price of loans from either a deterioration in the credit or an increase in a credit spread.

In the above example, the transaction could be structured to incorporate leverage. This would be achieved by embedding a higher face value of total return swap relative to the face value of the underlying floating rate cash investment in the note structure.

Leveraged total return loan swap indexed note

Issuer: AAA/AA rated institution

Principal amount: US$50 million

Maturity (years): The earlier of: (a) One year from commencement date. (b) The next succeeding payment date following default on the underlying credit asset.

Underlying credit asset: Loan to [XYZ Corporation] dated [15 March 1996]

Coupon: Leverage factor times margin plus leverage factor minus 1 times 3 month Libor plus margin payable quarterly on an actual/360 day basis.

Margin: [250] bps pa

Principal redemption: At par plus capital price adjustment subject to the minimum redemption level.

Minimum redemption level: 0%

Capital price adjustment: [Leverage factor] times principal amount times change (either positive or negative) in the price of the underlying credit asset. The price of the underlying credit asset is calculated as (current price – initial price)/initial price.

Initial loan price: 100 or face value

Current loan price: The [bid or offer] price of the underlying index as calculated by the calculation agent in accordance with the calculation method at 11.00 am (New York Time) two business days prior to each payment date.

Leverage factor: 8

Initial loan price: 100

Current loan price: The [bid or offer] price of the underlying index as calculated by the calculation agent in accordance with the calculation method at 11.00 am (New York Time) two business days prior to each payment date.

Calculation method:
- in the sole opinion of the calculation agent; or
- by dealer poll under which the calculation agent will poll at least four and no more than six dealers in the loan and utilize the quoted prices to determine an average price for the loan; or
- by reference to a screen or quote service.

Calculation agent: [Dealer]

In the above example structure which features 8 times leverage, the coupon is calculated as leverage factor times the coupon on the total return swap plus leverage factor minus 1 times Libor. This reflects the fact that the Libor payment on 1/leverage factor is effectively funded by the cash investment in the FRN. Figure 4.4 below demonstrates the construction and hedging of the leveraged note. Use of leverage requires caution as fluctuations in the value may have the effect of eroding the capital value of the underlying FRN in full. Consequently, in order to hedge the leveraged note it is necessary to combine the total return loan swap on the larger total principal with an option to avoid negative redemption value under the note. This aspect of leveraged structures is also relevant to leveraged versions of other types of credit linked notes, including credit default linked notes.

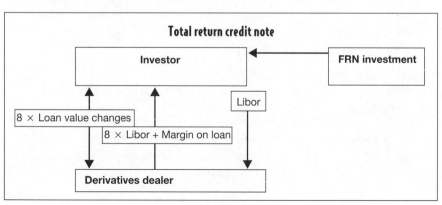

Fig 4.4

Shorting the loan market is traditionally difficult to achieve in the physical market because of the difficulty of borrowing non-government bonds for the purpose of creating the short sale. The ability to utilize embedded total return swaps to create the short position is advantageous in this respect.

Credit default notes

Credit default notes are primarily used to assume or reduce counterparty default exposure.

Credit default notes are primarily used to assume or reduce counterparty default exposure. Investors have traditionally used credit default structures to assume default exposure to generate premium income to enhance yield. However, structures which entail shifting of credit exposure, while less common, are also feasible.

Example

Credit default linked note

Issuer: AAA/AA rated institution
Principal amount: US$50 million
Term: Five years
Issuer price: 100 of face value
Issuer date: [Agreed date]
Coupon: Libor plus 150bps
Reference security: [Identified bond or loan of nominated borrower]
Principal security: [Identified bond or loan of nominated borrower]
Principal redemption: If no credit event has occurred before or as at maturity, then principal redemption is at face value. If a credit event has occurred before or as at maturity, then principal redemption is at par minus default payment.
Credit event: Any of the following with respect to nominated borrower:
■ failure to pay interest or principal on any senior debt security
■ event of bankruptcy
■ default on any senior unsecured obligation.

Default payment: Any of the following:
■ an agreed US$ amount equal to [40% of principal amount];
■ change in price of the reference security as between the issue date and date of agreed period after default as determined by a poll of selected dealers in the reference security;
■ payment of par or the price of the security at issue date in exchange for delivery of the defaulted reference security.

The example above sets out the details of a credit default note. The note structure depicted sets out a note linked to a single issuer credit. The credit default note is constructed by combining a cash investment with a default swap.

The notes are structurally created from the combination of a fixed interest security (fixed or floating coupon) and the entry by the investor into a credit default swap where the investor is the provider of default protection. The default payment or recovery rate is engineered into the principal redemption structure. The issuer enters into an offsetting default swap with a counterparty to eliminate its default risk position and generate a known cost of funds for the issuer.

The payment for the default swap is used to generate the return above the underlying interest rate on the credit default swap. In the event of default, the principal repayment to the investor is reduced by the amount of the default loss. The default loss can be calculated either as a fixed amount or an amount reflecting the actual recovery amount (calculated using changes in the value of the underlying bond following default using a dealer polling mechanism). The calculation mechanics are identical to those applicable to credit default swaps.

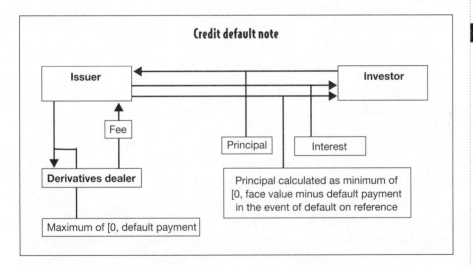

Credit default note

Fig 4.5

Figure 4.5 sets out the construction and hedging of a typical default note. The major advantages of the structure are as follows:

- provides yield enhancement in return for assuming the risk of default;
- allows utilization of credit risk assumption capacity which might not otherwise be capable of being utilized through the absence of available investments;

- separation of default risk and principal credit risk which are attributable to different underlying issuers;
- capped and known loss profile in the event of default.

The structure has some significant credit enhancement aspects. The fact that the credit default swap is embedded in the note which is purchased by the investor dictates that the performance obligation, to make the default payment in the case of default under the reference asset is fully collateralized. This results from the fact that, in the event of default, the issuer merely adjusts the payment to the investor reducing the principal repayment by the default obligation. This allows substitution of the credit of the issuer for the credit of the investor in the provision of default protection. This significantly broadens the range of institutions able to provide credit default protection through the unbundling of the assumptions of default risk from the actual counterparty credit risk of the party providing default protection. By extending the concept to the synthetic bond framework (discussed in detail in the next section), high quality collateral (government or high credit rated Aa/AA or better bonds) can be utilized to significantly increase the range of providers of default protection irrespective of the credit quality of the entity or person providing the protection.

Synthetic bonds

Synthetic bonds entail the issue of debt where the underlying credit risk exposure is created through a credit derivative transaction designed to replicate the characteristics of a fixed interest security issued by the underlying issuer.

These transactions are typically similar to asset repackaging – transactions involving the use of a special purpose repackaging vehicle. The central concept of these trust based structures is their ability to create trust receipts which represent repackaged cash flows which approximate a conventional bond which are sold to investors. The trust receipts are rated by one or more of the major rating agencies and the trust receipt is tradeable to facilitate liquidity. In essence, it is the conversion of asset swaps into public and tradeable securities.

Why repackage assets in collaterized loan obligations (CLOs)?

One of the largest deals in 1998 came from Deutche Bank.

Example

In July 1998, Deutche Bank issued its first CLO, CORE 1998–1, which parcelled loans to over 4,000 German corporates into Deutschmark and dollar denominated bonds worth a total of $2.4 billion.

Deutche Bank sold some DM4.26 billion of assets to a special purpose vehicle, liberating the regulatory capital it had held against them, worth at least 8% of the total (DM341 million). In place of that, Deutche will presumably only have to hold some DM75 million of capital, equivalent to 100% of the first loss reserve in the special purpose vehicle. The bank can recycle the freed up capital to originate more assets.

Banks want CLOs to be large, to increase the volume of loans they transfer, but the CLOs also have to be large, so the diversification can mitigate the impact of defaults on any of the underlying loans.

CLOs need to include loans with high enough yields to make the bonds attractive but, on the other hand, if the borrower's average credit quality is too low, the selling bank will have to retain such a large first loss exposure that the regulatory capital benefits disappear.

Key point

The theoretical advantages for banks in shifting loans off balance sheet and selling them to the capital markets are compelling, and the rapid growth in CLO issuance from $5billion in 1996 to $34billion in 1997 bears witness to the rapid acceptance of the idea.

Fig 4.6

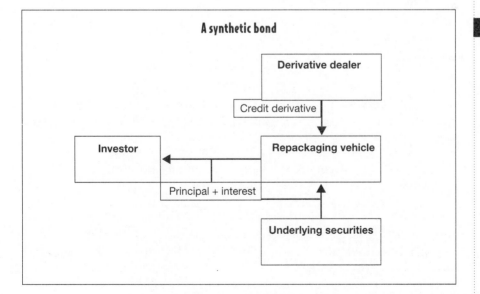

A synthetic bond

Derivative dealer

Credit derivative

Investor

Repackaging vehicle

Principal + interest

Underlying securities

Figure 4.6 illustrates the creation of a trust receipt on a structured note. The transaction entails the following steps:

- purchase of a security, in secondary markets;
- the lodgement of this security in the trust vehicle;
- the entry by the trust into a series of credit derivative transactions with a counterparty to engineer the required cash flow/risk profile. Typically, a conventional fixed or floating rate security can be engineered by combining it with the relevant credit derivative component to create the desired exposure;
- the trust then issues trust certificates representing the restructured cash flows of the security (combining the security and the derivative transactions) to the investor in return for payment of the face value;
- the trust collects all cash flows (principal, interest, and derivative settlements from the relevant counterparties) and passes them through the investor over the life of the transaction.

The credit rating of this trust arrangement is the rating of the bond plus the credit derivative transactions. The typical counterparty to the derivative transaction is an AAA or AA entity. The credit quality of the underlying security is selected by the issuer. The resulting transaction can be, at the option of the investor, issued as a rated or unrated security.

Advantages of the trust structure

The major advantages of this structure include:

- relative value considerations
- restructuring risk exposure
- credit selection
- liquidity
- flexibility.

These structures can provide significantly higher returns to the investors. The source of this enhanced return derives from:

- the ability to purchase undervalued securities in the secondary market;
- the avoidance of paying the issuer the required funding margin on a customized structured note issue.

The higher costs of the trust structure do not significantly affect the return as the majority of the costs are fixed on a per transaction basis and are substantially less than the enhanced return that can be generated from the identified sources.

Examples of synthetic bonds

There have been a number of examples of synthetic bonds. They fall into two categories: private repackaging or public bond issues.

The first of these has been the predominant form of transaction, in the US market, where trust structures, usually collaterized with high grade securities, have been combined with either total return loan swaps or credit default swaps to create customized exposures for investors.

> *There have been a number of examples of synthetic bonds. They fall into two categories: private repackaging or public bond issues.*

Public transactions are less common. The most notable examples of the second type of transaction involve JP Morgan who have issued two synthetic bonds: a $594 million transaction where the underlying credit exposure is to Walmart, the US retailing corporation; and a US$460 million transaction where the underlying exposure is to Walt Disney, the US entertainment company. The example below sets out the structure, including construction and hedging, of the Walmart synthetic bond.

Example of synthetic bond transaction

Example

Transaction: In late 1996, JP Morgan arranged an issue of a synthetic bond where the underlying credit was Walmart. The unique feature of the transaction was that it was completed independent of the participation of Walmart itself, insofar as Walmart did not issue the bonds nor guarantee the payment of interest and/or principal.

The transaction details were as follows:

Issuer: A special purpose trust
Underlying credit risk: Walmart
Amount: US$594 million
Maturity: Ten year final with amortization giving an average life of 5.8 years.
Yield: Treasury + 65bps

The transaction operates as follows:

- the investor purchases the note for value;
- the investor receives payment of interest and principal, provided Walmart is not in default;
- in the event of default, the investor receives repayment of principal equivalent to the recovery value of Walmart debt.

The relevant default event under the terms of this transaction is the default of Walmart under a reference credit obligation. In this particular transaction, a materiality provision was also incorporated in the definition of default requiring that the event of default will not have been deemed to have occurred unless the spread on Walmart public debt increased by a prespecified amount (believed to be 150bps pa).

The process of calculating the recovery value to establish the required market value of Walmart debt is also reasonably rigorous. It requires a dealer poll of five market makers in the reference obligations. The poll is to be conducted every two weeks for three months following default. The investor has the option of requiring either early redemption based on a dealer poll conducted as soon as possible after default, or redemption based on actual recovery value within an 18 month period. In the event that the 18 month period proves insufficient to derive actual recovery values, the recovery value is calculated using a dealer poll mechanism at the end of 18 months.

Construction of the synthetic bond

The construction of the synthetic bond is feasible in one of two ways.

Structure 1

This would entail collaterizing the issuing vehicle with floating rate securities purchased from the proceeds of the synthetic bond issue itself. The securities which generate floating returns (Libor + or – a margin) could be either floating rate securities or fixed rate bonds which are swapped using an interest rate swap. The issuing vehicle would simultaneously enter into a total rate of return swap where it pays a floating rate (Libor + or – a margin) and receives the return on the Walmart bonds or debt. The combined cash flows effectively create the cash flows and credit risk profile described in the example above.

Structure 2

This structure is identical to the first with the exception that the credit risk profile is created by the entry of the trust into a default swap whereby it receives a fee (payable per annum) in return for agreeing to make a payment based on the recovery rate following default of Walmart debt. The compensation received for assuming the default risk effectively enhances the return to the investor over and above the return on the collateral held in the trust.

The quality of the collateral in this case need only be of a credit quality sufficient to ensure that the rating of the structure equates to that of the underlying credit on a combined basis.

> **The issue of these synthetic bonds raises both a series of difficulties for the underlying credits and opportunities for intermediaries.**

The problems relate to the fact that the underlying credit effectively suffers a diminution in its control of the market in its own debt securities. For example, the Walmart transaction was priced at a yield spread to treasuries of 65bps (at issue) which compares favourably to publicly traded Walmart debt which trades at approximately 40bps spreads to treasuries. This discrepancy, which is partially attributable to inherent additional risks of the synthetic bond structure, may create pricing pressure as well as constraining the issuer's access to the underlying credit market.

The opportunities for intermediaries relate to the prospect of synthetically repackaged credit exposure in the form of bank debt or other types of financial transactions into a format which is capable of distribution in public markets to investors. The major advantage in this context is the opportunity to separate the issuer's desire to undertake the transactions from the creation of publicly tradeable obligation, allowing the investors to create the required exposure through the embedded credit derivative.

A closer look at leveraged credit derivatives

Now let's take a more in-depth look at leveraged credit linked notes.

> A Master Trust uses note proceeds to purchase US treasury securities and simultaneously enters into a swap with a bank, under which the bank pays the coupon flows on a loan portfolio, plus or minus price changes and receives floating interest cash flows from the trust. The investor receives the cash flows from the treasury security plus or minus the trust's net receipts under the swap with the bank.

Example

Reasons for doing such trades include the following :

■ some US investors, such as life insurers, who are required to use swaps for hedging purposes only, can gain the same economic result via the notes which are an allowable investment;

- the treasury collateral earns the note an investment grade rating;
- the investor earns the banking spreads built into the pricing of the loan portfolio and gets a leveraged upside with downside protection;
- the leverage can be tailored to match the investor's risk appetite;
- the bank sells off a large part of the credit risk in its portfolio.

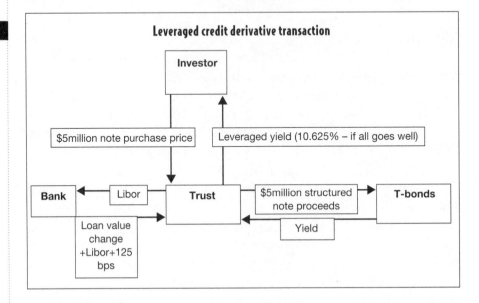

Fig 4.7

Leveraged credit derivative transaction

Figure 4.7 illustrates such a deal. In this deal, the note value is $5 million, while the underlying loans total $25 million, so the investor's upside is leveraged five times. Thus, if the value of the loans does change, the investor earns a return of 10.625 per cent (5 per cent from the treasury note + 5 times the 1.125 per cent spread on the swap with the dealer). However, the note is not without risks. Because of the leverage, a decline in the value of the loan portfolio by 2.125 per cent (caused, for example, by default) is enough to wipe out the investor's return for a year.

There are clearly dangers in badly structured leveraged products.

The use of leverage is very important at the systematic level. There are clearly dangers in badly structured leveraged products. But it is also the case that the use of leverage allows the banking system collectively to shift much larger amounts of credit risk into other market sectors. These purchases may, provided they have sufficient appetite for the risk and understanding of the dangers, in turn allow the banks to rebuild and extend their customer relationships by taking on more new business. This may, to some extent, allow banks to replace lending business lost to securitization. However, the growth of this technique will be restrained until the regulators recognize partial hedges.

Although securitization was underway before the imposition of the Basle Accord, its primary arena at that stage was in the mortgage-backed securities markets and commercial paper. The most rapid growth in securities took place after the imposition of the Basle Committee ratios forced banks to account properly for the cost of capital on loans. Now the use of leveraged credit linked notes may allow the banks to undo the effects of this by using these notes to pass on relatively large quantities of credit risk via moderate sized securities transactions, as illustrated in the Bistro transaction described below.

Glacier, Triangle and Bistro: credit linked pool structures

There have been several recent transactions in the credit linked note area which have pointed towards significant potential developments in the markets. The first of these was the *Glacier* transaction carried out by SBC Warburg (now known as UBS Warburg Dillon Read) in September 1997. Two tranches of floating rate notes were issued totalling $1.74 billion. These were backed by an initial collateral pool consisting of 130 credit linked notes, each of which was tied to the performance of a firm which has borrowed from SBC. SBC is required to maintain the weighted average credit rating of the pool, as well as a high level of industry and country diversification. Assets in the pool are cross-collateralized so that the bonds reflect the performance of all the notes in the pool. Although the bonds are non-callable, SBC retains the right to recall the underlying credit linked notes in the pool of collateral in order to reflect its current credit exposure. There is additional credit enhancement on the deal, derived from an element of excess spreads and a subordinated first-loss security. The total measure of the credit enhancement relating to the senior notes runs to 8.25 per cent of the nominal deal size. This level of protection is necessary because the identity of the obligors whose credit is being securitized is not known to the investor.

> Some interesting consequences flow from the fact that the Glacier transaction is structured to prevent knowledge of the borrower becoming available.

Key point

Glacier buys credit linked notes from SBC New York branch. Each note is a senior unsecured obligation of the bank, and is linked to the credit of a specific borrower. Glacier does not know the identity of the borrowers: SBC New York branch keeps a register identifying the borrowers, but does not disclose the identity to Glacier. Glacier's relationship is only with SBC New York branch, not with the borrower. Glacier has no rights in any obligation of any of the underlying borrowers. It has no rights to acquire from the bank any interest in any obligation of a borrower. Glacier and the trustee have no right to inspect any records of the New York branch. The entire operation, therefore, depends purely upon SBC's word for it that any given credit linked note is in default: no independent verification is possible.

This transaction was followed (in November 1997) by a transaction by CSFP called **Triangle** funding, and which is broadly similar in nature.

In December 1997, JP Morgan launched a $700 million transaction called **Bistro**. Under this transaction, a special purpose vehicle issued $460 million of AAA rated senior notes, together with $237 million of junior Ba2-rated notes, and $32 million of deeply subordinated 'equity' paper. The special purpose vehicle enters into a credit default swap with a notional principal value of $9.72 billion which is referenced to a portfolio of commercial loans, corporate and municipal bonds, and to counterparty credit exposure arising out of derivative contracts. The equity is funded through excess spread payable on the default swap over the course of the first five years of the transaction. A block of US treasuries further collateralizes the deal during the first five years of its life. Only when the treasury collateral is liquidated is Morgan entitled to offset portfolio losses against payments of interest and principal due on the bonds.

<table>
<tr><td>

Example

</td><td>

A summary of the Bistro – JP Morgan's leveraged CLO

Essentially, JP Morgan engaged in 300 credit default swaps written by JP Morgan, each of which conveys the risk that an investment grade corporate will default on its senior debt.

Investor's principal is forfeit to the extent of the defaults in the pool. The innovative feature of the deal was that the swaps represent a total exposure of $9.7 billion. In any CLO backed by high quality loans, the vast majority of the exposure can be rated AAA. Since an AAA rating denotes virtual risklessness, that portion of the deal achieves very little risk transfer for the selling bank, and is effectively just a more expensive way of funding the loan than the bank's normal borrowing.

JP Morgan's innovation was to split the AAA exposure into two tranches, and only issue the smaller, subordinated one. Morgan continues to fund the most senior section of the exposure on its balance sheet. Bond proceeds are

</td></tr>
</table>

invested in treasuries, which will repay the debt, so delinking it from JP Morgan's credit.

There is an extremely remote risk that so many of the underlying corporate borrowers will default that this super senior tranche is affected – but under the Federal Reserve Bank's forward looking approach to capital adequacy, JP Morgan's capital requirements are closer to the economic risk of assets than those of many other banks, and the senior tranche requires very little capital.

An interesting point to note in relation to the above, is that reference credits were publicly listed (unlike the Glacier transaction), and will remain constant throughout the life of the deal. Therefore Morgan, in fact, shorted some credits into the vehicle in anticipation of future exposure.

The effect of the overall structure is that the Bistro transaction is highly leveraged. Effectively, Morgan has bought protection for about 7 per cent of a $10 billion credit portfolio through the issue. Under the typical CBO/CLO transaction, the bank putting the transaction together retains exposure to the vast majority, often 90 per cent, of the economic loss likely to occur on the underlying collateral. With the Bistro transaction the reverse is the case. Morgan has sold off most of the first loss (with the possible exception of the $32 million equity). The assets, however, remained on Morgan's balance sheets. Morgan was not granted regulatory capital relief on the transaction. This is because the US Federal Reserve requires an exact match between the loan and the credit derivative, not merely as to obligor, maturity and seniority but also as to size. In other words, if we buy protection on $50 million, we are granted allowance to reflect reduction in exposure. This approach does not seem rational in my opinion.

Risks Associated with Credit Derivatives

Credit risk

Counterparty risk

Transaction risk

Liquidity risk

Compliance risk

Legal and regulatory risk

Pricing risk

Reputation risk

Credit risk

For the seller of the credit derivative the main risk is to the reference credit, and so for a credit default swap its risk is almost as though that reference asset itself were on the bank's balance sheet. For TROR swaps, however, the protection seller may be in a position (if the credit improves) where it is due to receive the appreciation from its counterparty. Therefore, in these transactions, the protection seller incurs credit risk for both the reference credit, and to a lesser extent, the counterparty.

> **As with other derivatives, credit derivatives pose multi-dimensional risks. Obviously the key risk is credit risk.**

Key point

As an example of how regulators see the risk, we consider the Federal Reserve. When it looks at a credit derivative, the Fed views the party that has transferred the credit risk as the 'beneficiary'. It views the party which has assumed the risk as the 'guarantor'. The guarantor has to hold capital against its exposure just as if it had exposure under other off balance sheet direct credit substitutes such as stand-by letters of credit. (For credit derivatives that include periodic payments for a change in the value of the credit, such as total rate of return swaps, the Fed lets the guarantor reduce the exposure by reducing the amount of depreciation paid to the beneficiary from the notional amount of the contract.) Under the Fed's rules, 100 per cent of the face amount of a guarantee is taken as the risk exposure. Other regulators' views are broadly similar on this.

It should be noted that the exact credit risk involved depends in part on how the trade settles. Depending on contract terms, if there is a default of the reference credit, protection sellers often choose to make a payment equal to the fall in value of the reference asset; or they can buy the asset at the notional contract amount and try to recover its value. The choice between cash settled and physical delivery default swaps raises important issues and debate has swung back and forth on this point.

The right answer depends on the circumstances. The main issues are whether the underlying is a loan or a bond, and whether there is a liquid market for the underlying or not. One participant took the view that as far as bonds were concerned: *"Four years ago every trade was physically delivered ... now, typically, if you've got a liquid underlying you would use cash settlement."*

However, if the market is not very liquid, there is generally a strong preference for delivery. Cash settled trading implies finding a fair value for the bond, and a seller of the bond could damage the price. If the underlying is a loan, on the other hand, other issues arise. Typically, where loan documentation provides for the assignment of loans to another buyer, it will do so on the basis that the assignment of loans 'will not be unreasonably withheld'. Yet one participant made the point that if the loan has been sold to a hedge fund, the agent bank might perfectly reasonably say that this was undesirable. In this case, perhaps, the fall-back alternative might be a sub-participation with no voting rights – but this would probably be unpalatable to the investor. One trader commented: *"A lot of trades I have seen have been done by people who either haven't addressed these issues or don't care about them."*

Counterparty risk

For the buyer of the credit protection, the primary risk is counterparty exposure. The protection buyer will lose money if its counterparty (i.e. the 'guarantor') does not fulfil its obligation. It follows that credit derivatives can never completely remove credit risk. This counterparty credit is similar to that of other derivative contracts, such as swaps, forwards and options. (Guarantors may also be exposed to counterparty credit risk if the trade is a total rate of return swap, since if the asset goes up in value they will expect to receive a payment from the counterparty.)

For the buyer of the credit protection, the primary risk is counterparty exposure.

For the beneficiary, if it is a bank, the Fed reduces the amount of capital it must hold for the credit. Assume that the Fed agrees that the credit protection is enough to allow treatment of the derivative as a guarantee. Then the bank may assign the asset to the guarantor's risk category: for example, 20 per cent if the guarantor is a bank from an OECD country.

One market participant argues that this treatment is a good deal stiffer than it looks. The policy neglects the fact that if you buy DEM 100 million of protection on Daimler risk from Barclays it requires both Daimler and Barclays to fail. Providing there is no correlation between protection seller and the underlying credit (an important provision, as those who bought protection on Korean credits from Korean banks will attest) the combined probability of the two failures is quite low.

Counterparty risk is found from the mark to market value of the credit derivative and an 'add-on' factor representing potential future exposure. Under the Basle rules, the add-on factor is a specified percentage of the notional amount, depending on the type and maturity of the deal. To work out a capital charge for the counterparty risk for credit derivatives, an appropriate add-on factor is needed. However, the current matrix of add-on factors in the Basle Accord does not include a specific factor for credit or other derivatives for which the underlying transaction is a debt instrument. The Fed has decided that the equity add-on factors are to be used when the reference asset is an investment grade instrument (or equivalent), or where the reference asset is unrelated but well secured by high quality collateral. The commodity add-on factor is to be used when the reference asset is either below investment grade (or equivalent) or is unrated and unsecured. The Bank of England approach is generally to use the equity add-on.

The treatment just mentioned would apply if the guarantee is limited in any material way. This might happen if the credit derivative agreement adopts a restrictive definition of a credit event, or if it sets a materiality threshold that requires a large loss to happen before the guarantor must pay. In that case the protection is severely weakened.

In effect, the rules require regulators to make a case-by-case decision on whether a particular credit derivative has effectively transferred the credit risk. This approach has created uncertainty about the regulatory treatment of a particular transaction; but it is hoped that, as documentation is standardized, this problem will diminish.

Transaction risk

In a credit derivative the extent of credit transfer depends on the specific deal (unless it is done under the newly introduced ISDA documentation, and even here there is a good deal of scope for negotiation). One credit derivative, therefore, can transfer a much higher share of credit risk than another. For example, some credit derivatives pay out only when a previously defined default or downgrade occurs. Others might make a payment only for the loss in value beyond a threshold. Some might specify a reference asset that is similar, but not identical, to an asset the bank owns. Hence we need to look carefully at the correlation between an owned asset and the reference asset specified in the credit derivative.

The problem is that no two trades are the same, there is bid/offer risk in the documentation, and basis risk in the documentation – if you have ten credit events when you sell protection, and only one when you buy, you are setting yourself up for problems. Negotiation for trades still takes days if not weeks, deals unravel all the time.

A point arises here that there might be a specific problem where the trigger events differ between derivatives bought and sold. This is a risk which traditional reporting systems are not well adapted to identify.

Key point

> If the credit protection proves to be illusory, because the credit reporting system has failed to capture the risks fully, the total risk might be far greater than the firm ever intended to run.

Firms' management may optimistically believe that all credit risks are safely hedged and therefore end up taking bigger gross positions than they previously would have done. The new world of credit risk protection may create an artificial sense of security. One of the worrying trends is that the market is getting rid of materiality clauses. What then happens in the case of technical default? Does the trade just collapse?

Finally, credit derivatives may provide protection against loss on loans to the reference credit for a shorter period than the remaining maturity of the underlying. This is quite an important point, and one which we will return to, as there has been a good deal of argument about how to treat such a case.

Liquidity risk

For firms holding credit derivatives strictly for hedging, liquidity risk is relatively unimportant. For example, consider a bond issuer who uses a credit option to hedge its future costs of borrowing. Because the option will be structured to expire on the borrowing date, the bond issuer will simply hold the option until expiry.

In contrast, liquidity risk is important for issuers of credit derivatives and for users of credit derivatives who plan to close out their position before the contract matures.

Key point

> It is quite clear from the recent Russian default on domestic and public debt, and the Japanese banking crisis, as well as the domino effect on the emerging markets, Asia and Latin America, that there is still significant liquidity risk.

During the devaluation of the rouble, September 1998, there were no offers to be seen anywhere on default protection on any Russian sovereign debt.

At the start of the Russian crisis, three month Russian protection (default swap) bids, were trading at 2500bps pa, i.e. buyers of default protection where prepared to pay 25 per cent per annum to protect themselves against Russian bonds defaulting. One brave seller was willing to provide protection for 35 per cent. Very soon after this, Russian sovereign dollar denominated debt was trading at 35 per cent close to default. There were no offers in the market. Liquidity in default swaps dried up quickly for most emerging market default protection.

Compliance risk

Because credit derivative instruments are new and evolving, there are uncertainties about some legal issues, the appropriate regulatory capital and reporting treatment, as well as other regulatory issues. For default swaps and credit linked notes with embedded default swaps, the definition of a default and the determination of the payout following default are major issues to be thought through. We return to some of these risks in the next chapter.

> **Compliance risk** is the risk arising from violations of laws, or rules and regulations.

Definition

Legal and regulatory risk

Another source of risk for credit derivative users is legal risk.

> **Legal risk** is the possibility that a derivative contract may be deemed illegal or unsuitable.

Definition

In part, the risk here is because in several countries there is still some uncertainty about the status of these instruments. Should credit derivatives be treated as securities, commodities, swaps, or insurance products?

The distinction is important in some countries, such as the US, because these contracts are regulated by different agencies and under different terms. Suppose that a firm enters a credit swap contract in the US. If the regulatory status changes and the contract is subsequently regarded as a security, it would then be under the jurisdiction of the SEC. Since SEC regulations require additional disclosure, the contract could be considered illegal. A change in regulatory status could therefore potentially invalidate previously established derivative transactions.

A similar risk arises from the question of whether a country's legal framework will recognize the instrument. A well-known example of this problem was the swap defaults by Hammersmith and Fulham and other municipalities in the UK, following a legal decision that they were not capable of entering swaps because their governing legal framework did not recognize the instruments.

Pricing risk

This is the risk that a firm may systematically misprice a product line. Examples have been seen in other derivatives markets – such as the recent case where NatWest Markets systematically mispriced some of its interest rate option books. Clearly, there are potentially major problems in pricing credit risk accurately on a portfolio basis, which we discuss in Chapter 8.

Key point

> The absence of historical data on defaults, and on correlation between default events, complicates the precise measurement of risk.

In default swaps, the seller of credit protection will tend to make infrequent payments. However, when they have made them, those payments can be large. Also, because of the limited liquidity, dealers may find it hard to price deals and to hedge exposures. So dealers may find themselves more vulnerable to high volatilities of anticipated cash flows than is the case with other financial derivative products.

The data in credit derivatives is not like interest rate or foreign exchange rates. Default rates on loans are partly driven by the management decisions of the banks: they are not purely exogenous.

Clearly, this has an important bearing on the modelling of loan risk and it is a point which seems not to have been widely enough considered.

Reputation risk

There are obvious potential pitfalls with novel instruments using complex and unfamiliar documentation. This applies particularly to certain classes of credit derivative which are often not so well understood, for example, basket trades. A participant recalled one instance of being offered a note which was issued linked to Asian credits. If any one of these defaulted, the investor ended up with those bonds. The paper was being marketed as an 'Asian investment grade basket note' which was hardly an accurate title.

> Credit derivatives with leveraged payoff profiles pose particular reputation risks.

Key point

Examples include binary default swaps, which require the protection seller to make a fixed payment upon default, without regard to any recovery on the reference asset. Clearly, firms' compliance teams will need to be sure that transactions are appropriate, and that the counterparty will be able to fulfil its obligation under the terms of the contract.

Collaterized Bond Obligations (CBOs)

Introduction

Almost any asset can be sliced and diced by Wall Street to resemble a fixed income bond: revenues linked to the future sales of Tequila, future royalties on David Bowie songs, the proceeds from the sale of second-hand Russian cars. The asset backed market is exploding, and fuelling the growth is the tremendous appetite for yield. The reason the market is so hungry for yield is that returns on fixed income bonds have come down (historically), interest rates are low and credit spreads are low. It is therefore difficult to get an adequate return in the traditional fixed income market.

Junk debt high yielding junk bonds have never been hotter: more than $46 billion were issued in the first half of 1997, in 1996 the total was $65 billion, in 1995 the record was set at $67.7 billion.

CBOs are a means of repackaging low quality assets into investment grade debt.

Key point

CBOs were used in the late 1980s by Drexel Burnham Lambert to package parts of its inventory. These CBOs, in turn, were sold to Drexel managed mutual funds.

Drexel closed its doors in the 1980s after being implicated in the Ivan Boesky insider trading scandal. As the US economy plunged headlong into recession, many of the leveraged management buy-outs around which several of the structures were designed filed for bankruptcy. Executive Life insurance in California also put bonds it owned into CBOs. When default rates soared in the 1990s, holders of these securities suffered huge losses.

Eight years later CBOs are still controversial. Supporters hail the CBO as the grandfather of the asset backed market as we know it today. They maintain that the way in which CBOs were used to repackage junk debt into high yielding investment grade paper was truly groundbreaking. It enabled US savings and loans institutions to generate extra yield off their commercial books. Critics say that CBOs enabled bankers to offload bottom of the heap credits that they could not shift elsewhere.

Many of the CBOs trading today are much more leveraged than the 'worst' structured note. In 1994, when Greenspan raised interest rates, holders of the structured notes were badly stung. Some structured notes were leveraged several hundreds of times over – these produced the most yield. In comparison, some CBOs are leveraged 1,000 times and more.

Replication

Replication is close to impossible – even worse, there are more structured risks in CBOs than there were in the structured notes. Unlike structured notes, it is almost impossible to reverse engineer the CBOs without incurring a basis risk.

Key point

- The CBO has no 'fungible' building blocks
- It is difficult to re-engineer the future cash flows.

Nor is there a liquid secondary market, so prices are not very transparent. Of course, bankers are not keen to draw parallels between structured notes and CBOs. For one thing, an obviously concerned Greenspan has already warned dealers to expect an official response to any further 'irrational exuberance' in the asset markets. Another factor is that investors are far more sophisticated in terms of understanding the structures and in terms of risk measurement and management.

Not so long ago, the innovation behind bringing a security to the market centered around fees it could generate or the exploitation of one-off arbitrage opportunities. The CBO issuance especially was a function of the spread between the high yield and the investment grade markets and the availability of equity to finance it. Now the talk on Wall Street is to use CBOs as a complementary vehicle to credit derivatives. Until there are more tools to hedge credit risks, bondholders will remain keen on the idea of removing high risk credits from their portfolios by packing them in a CBO.

Investors are realizing that the only thing that counts in today's financial markets is the 'search for yield'.

Investors and yield pick up

Tightening credit spreads are forcing investors much further out along the credit risk curve than they would otherwise be comfortable with. Investors are realizing that the only thing that counts in today's financial markets is the 'search for yield'. Italian ten year sovereign paper used to trade 700bps, over equivalent German Bunds, now the spread is 52bps.

In Japan, domestic pension funds have made promises of a minimum 5 per cent annual return. However, the stock market is collapsing (or recently has actually collapsed, and is struggling to fight back as of the end of 1998). In the Japanese bond market you can only get about 1 per cent at its highest point. In the US, the gap between bond yields and the nominal rate of gross domestic product growth is at a ten year low – about 100bps.

The future will be shaped by issues such as EMU, Japanese government intervention in a failing financial system, and deflation. It is unlikely that high yields will occur again particularly in Europe.

Financial engineering

Investment bankers have to engineer securities which will deliver high yields that the market is hungry for. On the other hand, there are tightening credit spreads.

> **Key point**
>
> The challenge for investment bankers is to:
>
> ■ build enough of a premium to adequately reflect the extra risks involved; and
> ■ ensure that investors can price these extra risks adequately.

CBOs are a good way to bridge the gap. In the first half of 1997, $8 billion of CBOs were marketed, the same amount as were sold in 1996. Rather than take it on their own balance sheets, bankers are originating, then passing on credit exposure via CBOs to insurance companies and fund managers. This is a radical departure from the 'old way' of doing banking. In the past, banks took on the credit risk and incorporated it into their own books. US ratings agency, Standard & Poor's rated more than $4.5 billion worth of CBOs towards the end of 1996. They averaged two deals a month in 1997. As much as $22 billion in total is waiting to be rated by Moody's Investor Services and Standard & Poor's.

Market size

There are no official data since CBOs are privately placed deals. As of March 1997, traders believe that there are 50 structures worth more than $12 billion. In January 1997, Capital Markets Assurance

Corporation of New York (CAPMAC) provided the first financial guarantee to a CBO consisting of Asian corporate bonds. In March 1997, Nomura launched a structure aimed exclusively at Japanese retail investors backed by US investment grade bonds.

New players in the CBO market

Merril Lynch, UBS (SBC Warburgs), and DMG have all expanded into this area. It is not hard to see why. One CBO issue generated $18.5 million in arrangement and placement fees on a $200 million deal. The breakdown in this CBO deal is as follows.

$3.1 million in placement fees
$2 million in structuring fees
$1.4 million a year in investment management fees.

Underlying securities

To date, much of the paper has come out of the US junk bond market and, to a lesser extent, the emerging markets of Latin America. Key players believe these structures will shift to Europe where there is distressed German and French debt.

The CBO principle

The principle behind CBOs is quite simple. The issuer is a bankruptcy remote special purpose vehicle, frequently rated AAA. It buys a pool of assets which it then uses to collaterize a series of securities.

Key point

> By subordinating or ranking each series (or tranche) of securities in terms of seniority, the issuer protects the senior tranches from bankruptcy risk. The junior tranches are responsible for shouldering that risk.

Bottom tranche

The bottom tranche seldom has a coupon and rarely attracts a rating. It behaves very much like equity with a similar risk/return profile. However, the bottom tranche is pivotal to the deal. It determines the level of protection (and credit rating) of the senior tranches.

Senior tranches

To get an AAA rating, the senior subordinated securities must be collateralized approximately 1.5 times. An issuer that sources $500 million of assets would be allowed to issue no more than $330 million AAA rated securities against the pool: $500/1.5 = $330. The same issuer would have to place $170 million of junior subordinated debt to get the deal done. If the issuer was willing to settle for AA rating, the ratio goes down to 1.25. Now they can issue $400 million of senior tranche and $100 million of junior tranche debt.

The question remains as to how to structure the portfolio to give enough of a return to the junior tranche. According to the head of one of the US's largest CBO players: *"You know exactly where you can place AAA rated Libor plus paper. The problem is finding buyers with the risk appetite to take the rump. Quite simply, until you pre-place the bottom rung, you don't have a deal – the only way to get investment grade ratings on the senior tranches is to source and sell the junior tranche and thus guarantee at least some credit enhancement."*

Unlike most vanilla debt origination operations, CBO issuers rarely go long for an entire deal in the hope of placing junior tranches at a later date. However, placement is not impossible. The senior subordinated securities may come in around 12–20bps over Libor. The junior tranches may generate annual yields in excess of 25–30 per cent.

In 1996, Moody's Investor Services' speculative grade total return index outperformed US Treasuries by 13 per cent and some emerging market CBOs have posted annual gains of up to 50 per cent on the back of the strong rally in the emerging markets.

The party that buys the junior tranche of the CBO thinks like a pure equity trader. Some clients include special opportunity fund managers, insurance funds and banks.

Key point

Rather than put a pool of assets on the balance sheet which would result in regulatory capital hit on the entire principal amount, a bank could get essentially the same exposure by the purchase of a smaller amount of CBO junior tranche.

The junior tranche of the CBO guarantees the level of protection to the senior tranche and thus affords them their credit rating. The size of the tranche is determined by the losses that the asset pool is likely to sustain from defaults.

The junior tranche must be:

- large enough to absorb any expected losses to protect the senior tranche; but
- small enough for the issuer to place.

The size of the junior tranche has to do with:

- the probability of default
- the expected recovery value once a 'credit event' occurs
- correlation.

Probability of default

A standard method for estimating probability of default is to use historical data to compute the probability of default, but which data do you use?

The methodology has a lot to do with the way default data is interpreted. For example, the current annual default rate in the junk market is 1.6 per cent, well below the 3.6 per cent historical average. In 1991, one in every ten sub investment grades defaulted on public debt issues.

It is very difficult to collect data on individual issues. You need to compute the correlation of 'default events'. So many investors use a basket as a proxy.

An emerging market CBO might be pegged to the JP Morgan Brady bond fixed rate index. A US domestic junk bond CBO might be pegged to the Merrill Lynch high yield bond index.

> It is very difficult to collect data on individual issues. You need to compute the correlation of 'default events'.

This is a generally accepted practice. But there are substantial basis risks. The quoted default rates on benchmark indices are about 1.5–2 per cent. Moody's put the probability of default on a portfolio of sub investment grade corporates over the next three years at 8 per cent rising to 40 per cent over the next ten years. The benchmark index would have a probability of default of $(1-(1-2\%)^3)=5.88\%$ in three years $(1-(1-2\%)^{10})=18.29\%$ in ten years.

The differences are due to the fact that the indices are composed of very young bonds. Junk bond issuance has risen from almost nothing in 1991 to about 500 deals in 1996. New issues have start up capital at hand to protect them from bankruptcy during their first years.

Call risk

High yield bonds tend to be called if their quality and credit rating improve. On average, as many junk debt issues are likely to be called during the first ten years as are likely to default. Holding them in a CBO is an asymmetrical bet: the winners get called and the losers default.

Credit risk models

It is much more difficult to model credit risk than it is to model market risk. It is much more dangerous to make inferences from historical default data. The problem is compounded by the assumptions dealers make on default rates and the recovery rates. For example, some dealers assume that default rates are the same regardless of rises in interest rates. So the main question is: are default rates independent of interest rates? Are they correlated with interest rates? If so, how?

Sensitivity to interest rates

The senior tranche of the CBO is more sensitive to interest rates than the junior tranche. By the time you get to the bottom of the barrel, it is pretty much a story thing. Either the credit structure of the CBO is going to survive or they are going to default. This is not going to be determined by a 25bps rise in rates.

Fixed coupons

Most sub investment grade paper carries fixed coupons. So dealers tend to issue fixed rate CBOs. Asset swappers cannot offer investors a fixed to floating swap overlay on the CBO. It is almost impossible to determine the cash flows of the underlying basket in advance. CBOs are completely illiquid esoteric structures with unique risk profiles. Issuers tend to embed an out of the money interest rate cap into the structure so that the residual interest rate risk is just the difference between the cap's strike and the current Libor rates. For example, with dollar Libor at around 4.75 per cent, an eight and a half year cap struck at 7 per cent might cost the CBO around $3.5 million. An at the money cap might cost $8.5 million.

The sweetener

The demand for the junior tranches usually comes from buyers seeking floating rate exposures. The sweetener often comes in investment management fees. The investment management involves the day-to-day handling of the portfolio, collecting coupons etc. This fee is contingent on an investor agreeing on 50 per cent of the junior tranchee. The fee can be as high as 70–100bps a year. On a $200 million deal with eight and a half years, this is a substantial sum.

Example

A sample CBO deal

- Approximately $200 million collateral
- High yield 35% emerging market collateral
- Interest rate cap of hedge if Libor rises above 8%
- Structuring fee: 100bps
- Collateral management fees: 75-100bps per year
- Securities issued:

Size ($ million)	Rating	Maturity (years)	Coupon	Placement fee (in bps)
50	AAA	7	Libor+35	62.5
110	Aa2	12	Libor+80	87.5
10	Baa2	12	US T+275	275
30	Unrated	12	n/a	500

Collateral pool:
$200 million of high yield and emerging market debt, largely B rated

$142 million – US domestic high yield
$22 million – fixed income emerging markets
$31 million-floating rates emerging markets
$5 million – cash

VaR analysis on the underlying basket:
For one year, 99% confidence interval on the underlying assets
on $142 million US high yield = $10.8 million
on $22 million fixed rate emerging = $14.4 million
on $31 million floating rate emerging = $19.5 million

VaR (before correlation effects) = $44.7 million
VaR (after correlation effects) = $38.3 million

For the four year duration of the eight-and-a-half year structure, the VaR is the square root of the duration, 2*$38.3 = $76.7 million.

CBOs are not readily amenable to VaR analysis

Applying VaR to the CBO in the example above reveals that there is a significant chance, about 1 in 20, that the entire subordinated notes would become valueless over the life of the structure and that a portion of the senior tranche would become impaired as well. Given a four year holding period, the CBO would expect to lose $76 million once every 100 days. Such a loss would wipe out investors in the unrated as well as the Baa2 tranche and also affect those in the Aa2 tranche.

Critics argue that this is 'toxic waste' bundled with a little extra yield. The real test will come when a CBO has to absorb a default. Moody's issued a grim warning in its 1996 review of the markets. While total defaults were at an all-time low (27 issuers defaulted on $5.4 billion worth of public debt), the quality of new issuance deteriorated rapidly.

More than 70 per cent of the recorded $67 billion speculative grade investments issued in 1998 came with a ranking of B or below. Before the meltdown of 1990, only 43 per cent were similarly rated. Moody's concluded that the significant supply of lower rated paper will put upward pressure on default rates through 1997 and beyond.

Within 24 hours of South Korean steel and construction group Hanbo collapsing on 23 January 1997 spreads on two year paper moved up by 30bps and the country's three largest banks were downgraded.

Coupon enhanced credit linked SIRES (CLSs)

CLSs have the following main characteristics:

- they are trusts with the return of the underlying collateral enhanced through default provision linked to the issue;
- they pay higher coupon than the reference underlying bond. Typically the yield enhancement is 30–100bps pa;
- they carry more default risk than the reference underlying bond. In the event of default, or if the underlying credit trades to a default level, coupon payment will cease and the SIRES will redeem to zero;
- the investor gives up the expected recovery value of a defaulted bond in exchange for enhanced yield if solvency is maintained;
- they have maturities of three to seven years;
- the reference collateral is identical to the reference bond for the default provision;
- the underlying reference bond may be of a different currency denomination than the CLS.

Application of credit linked SIRES (CLSs)

CLSs have the following main applications:

- they suit investors who hold bonds to maturity. For investors who purchase bonds with a reasonably strong view against default, CLSs provide enhanced return over the straight bond purchase;
- they are excellent vehicles to monetize recovery value. An investor who feels the expected recovery value of the underlying reference bond is minimal can forgo the recovery value and achieve enhanced returns (for example, subordinated issues of high quality issuers may fit this category).

Example

XYZ five year bond

Expected cumulative probability of default: 7.00%
Expected recovery value upon default: 40.00%
Expected value foregone: 7%*40% = 2.80%

CLS coupon enhanced per annum: 1.00%
Coupon enhancement present value: 4.20%

Conclusion:
Purchase CLS because present value of a coupon enhancement exceeds expected foregone value.

The flaw in the above argument is that, if the bond defaults after two years, say, you will not receive the expected coupon enhancement, i.e. they do not all default after five years – some default sooner.

Price sensitivity of credit linked SIRES

The price sensitivity of the CLS is typically three to four times that of the underlying reference issue. They will move in the same direction but create a much bigger movement. This is because the CLS can go down to a zero redemption, but the reference underlying issue will still have a recovery value.

Investors can consider that a CLS is created by selling 'default' options. These options are currently out of the money. As they move in the money, their value increases quite rapidly. The strike is the 'trigger' level shown at the principal redemption. Since the investor is short the options, the value of the CLS will decline rapidly.

Key point

The higher price sensitivity of these notes confirms that they are not trading instruments. They are meant to be held to maturity.

Some coupon enhanced linked note trade examples

Coupon enhanced ABC 7.45% 1 February 1998 Linked note (as of 14 November 1994)

Issuer: SIRES
Underlying trust asset: ABC 7.45% of 1 February 1998
Principal amount: $5 to $10 million
Settlement date: Two weeks
Maturity date: 9 February 1998
Price: Par
Coupon: 9.45% (Current ABC yield + 0.80%)
Coupon payment dates: 9 February and 9 August, short first coupon
Principal redemption: Par, unless default provision is activated
Default provision: If, at any time during the life of this note, ABC Inc. fails to make a payment due on the ABC 7.45% of 1 February 1998, interest payments will cease and the structured note will be redeemed at zero.
Current ABC yield: UST 8.125% 2/98 + 1.22%

In this note, the investor enhances the yield of ABC by 0.80% per annum, on a SIRES with ABC as collateral, as long as ABC does not default on the underlying security.

Basket credit linked notes

A basket credit linked note pays an enhanced coupon over the average yield of a basket of three or more underlying reference bonds.

The major advantage of a basket credit linked note is that the default event will not result in a complete loss of principal. Instead, the investor will be delivered an amount of the defaulted bond equal to 80 per cent of the CLN face value. Therefore, the investor only relinquishes 20 per cent of the expected recovery value upon default.

Basket credit linked notes typically have reference bonds that are close to maturity, but need not necessarily be of the same country or industry. Other banks offer basket notes which pay zero on a credit event. This, in my opinion, is foolish trade, since very few defaults result in a 100 per cent loss of principal. Even the current Russian default on senior unsecured foreign debt only resulted in a 70 per cent loss.

Example

Coupon enhanced basket credit linked note (as of 14 November 1994)

Issuer: To be determined, single A or better

Principal amount: $5 to $10 million

Settlement date: Two weeks

Maturity date: 30 June 1998

Price: Par

Coupon: Six month Libor + 1.35%, Act/360

Coupon payment dates: 30 June and 30 December, short first coupon

Principal redemption: Par, unless default provision is activated

Default provision: If, at any time during the life of the note, one of the bonds in the basket defaults on principal or interest payment due, the investor will receive 80% of the notional amount (face value) of the defaulted bond or any other bond in the basket, and the issuer will have no further obligation to repay principal or interest.

Basket:

Bonds	Maturity	Yield
Boise Cascade	December 2000	L+68
American Airlines	July 1999	L+98
US Steel	July 1999	L+39
Korean Dev Bank	June 1999	L+40
Bank of China	March 2000	L+58
Average yield:		L+61

In the note in the above example, the investor earns six month Libor + 1.35 per cent semi-annually representing an enhancement of 0.74 per cent over the current basket yield. The investor takes additional risk but in the event that one of the bonds in the basket defaults.

Regulatory Capital for Credit Derivatives

Introduction

Consistent with the developing nature of the market, there are currently no definite guidelines on the treatment of credit derivatives for regulatory purposes. Users of credit derivatives must, consequently, evaluate appropriate regulatory capital treatment independently. This is mostly done by

The emergence of a market in credit derivatives has been greeted with cautious support by regulators.

drawing analogies with more conventional instruments for which a well developed regulatory framework already exists.

The emergence of a market in credit derivatives has been greeted with cautious support by regulators. This support is predicated on recognition of the significant potential benefits that these new instruments offer to financial institutions in the management of credit risk. There have been a number of official pronouncements on the regulation of credit derivatives. The US Office of the Comptroller of the Currency has produced documents that provide guidance for bank end users of credit derivatives, but they do not state a definite regulatory position. The Bank of England has also published a consultative paper on credit derivatives.

When reviewing the regulatory framework, it is important to note that regulators of other capital market participants, primarily insurance company regulators, have also begun to review the treatment of credit derivatives. The attitude of the National Association of Insurance Companies (NAIC) has been to not discourage the use of credit derivatives either to hedge credit exposure within investment portfolios or as a form of investment (for example, in the form of credit derivatives). It is understood that the NAIC Securities Valuation Office is in the process of finalizing its policies in relation to rating structured note investments where the payoff is linked to credit derivatives. It is expected that the treatment is likely to be similar to that of public rating agencies.

> **Key point**
>
> It is quite clear that this is a market where there are still relatively small volumes of transactions. In very large part, this can be attributed to the fact that the legal and regulatory aspects of these transactions have not yet been finalized.

It is clear that much work has to be done: for example, the Bank of England has been working on a paper which will reflect an update of its

1996 paper. The Commission Bancaire in France has produced a paper which follows up its original draft recommendation of 1997. The German position, it seems, is that almost nothing has been published officially, and to the extent that German banks are active in the market-place, it appears that they are active primarily through London or New York. Other centres, such as Spain, Italy and other European countries, appear at this point to be awaiting a lead from other countries.

In the Japanese case, of course, the regulators can be forgiven for placing a higher priority on other matters, such as saving the remains of the banking system. However, despite the fact that the global picture is still by no means settled, enough has been set down by various regulators to raise a number of issues, some of which will be discussed here. However, it is important first to outline the regulatory issues that are at the forefront of the debate, and to take a brief look at the typical way total rate of return swaps and credit default swaps are regarded, i.e. to carry out an informal regulatory analysis.

The regulatory issues

The issues in relation to the regulatory requirements of credit deriva-tives revolve around the treatment of these instruments for regulatory capital. There are several distinct issues:

- whether derivatives should be included in either the banking or the trading books of financial institutions;
- the treatment of the *underlying* reference credit in the books of the entity seeking protection or transferring the economic risk of the credit assets;
- the treatment of the *underlying* reference credit in the books of the entity providing protection or acquiring the economic risk of the credit assets;
- the treatment of the counterparty risk on the credit derivative itself.

The regulatory treatment problems vary in relation to credit spread products, total rate of return loan swaps, and default swaps.

Credit spreads are analogous to positions in the underlying assets (long or short securities in a risky asset and an offsetting position in a risk free security). This decomposition should logically allow the market risk of the position to be determined and the regulatory market risk capital requirement to be calculated. The counterparty credit risk should be derived by analogy with interest rate products. This would dictate that the counterparty risk is treated as the mark to market of the position plus the usual add-on factor for interest rate products.

Total rate of return loan swaps and default swaps are inherently more complex, reflecting the transfer of the credit risk of the underlying credit assets. This chapter will concentrate on the treatment of total return swaps and credit default swaps.

Regulatory analysis

The position adopted by the regulators is still evolving but some guidance is available from the discussion papers published by both the OCC and the Bank of England.

Total return loan swaps

Total return swaps are to be treated in the bank's trading books. The treatment is conditional on the liquidity of the underlying asset rather than the issue of the isolation of the credit risk. In order to qualify for trading book treatment, the dealer institution must be able to mark to market the underlying reference asset. Where the liquidity of the underlying asset is not demonstrable, the swap will be included in the banking book.

> The ability to include the transaction in the bank's trading book has significant capital benefits as traded instruments are risk capital weighted at between 0.25 per cent and 1.6 per cent of the notional value of the transaction compared to 8 per cent if included in the banking book.

Key point

To put it a little more simply, if the swap ends up in the banking book, and if the swap is a $50 million notional, you need to put up $4 million capital reserve for that position compared to between $125,000 and $800,000 if it ends up in the trading book. A significant saving, the difference in capital can be put to much better use (invested), hence earning a better return than just the risk free rate.

Where the transaction qualifies for inclusion in the trading book, the total return swap is decomposed into synthetic long or short positions in the underlying asset and an offsetting position in an FRN for the interest payments. There is an additional charge for counterparty credit risk on the swap.

The essential issue under this approach is whether the specific risk charge on the synthetic position in the swap is able to offset against a position in the asset (i.e. the holding being hedged). The offset is allowed where the reference asset is identical as between the physical holding and the swap.

Where the reference asset is of the same asset class but not identical to the asset being hedged, the general risk charge on the two positions are offsetting within the general risk calculations (leaving either zero or a small general market risk charge) but there is no reduction in the specific charge.

Maturity mismatches may be allowed with shorted dated swaps being utilized to hedge a longer dated position in the physical asset. The regulators are divided on this issue: the Bank of England accepting maturity mismatches whereas US regulators require the maturities to be matched under the 'virtual complete credit protection' doctrine (see the US, Bank of England and SFA positions later on in this chapter).

With the total return swap, the position is more complex with the following options of treatment available:

1 If the swap exactly offsets another position in the same asset, the issuer risk on both positions is exactly offset leaving only counter-party risk on the swap.

2 If the swap does not exactly match the underlying asset, then whether or not it is recognized as reducing exposure will depend on how closely it matches. There is uncertainty about the treatment under this scenario with the suggested treatment being that of a guarantee or letter of credit with the risk weight being reduced to that of the counterparty. The matching process requires satisfaction of the following criteria:
   ■ *Asset* – the correlation between the asset being hedged and the reference asset underlying the swap.
   ■ *Maturity match* – correspondence between maturities of the positions.

3 If the swap is not hedging an underlying position, then:
   ■ if the swap entails a *short position*, it is ignored;
   ■ if the swap entails a *long position*, it is treated as a direct credit substitute and the risk weight is that of the reference asset.

There is also the issue of the counterparty credit risk against which capital must also be held. The replacement cost of the contract is self-evident although absence of liquidity may make it difficult to establish the true market value of the contract. There is uncertainty about the add-on factor for potential future exposure. The regulators appear to favour the equity products add-ons for total return swaps referenced to bonds.

Credit default swaps

For credit default products (credit default swaps), the regulatory positions appear to require inclusion in the banking book. If protection is sold, the exposure is treated as a direct credit substitute and the risk weight is that of the reference asset.

The criteria which must be met are as follows:

- the asset match must demonstrate high correlations;
- the protection must cover the full life of the underlying asset;
- the payments structure must have minimal uncertainties. Fixed payment and physical delivery options are regarded as certain payment structures. Par less recovery rate structures are regarded as uncertain structures.

Where all three criteria are met, the capital charge will be recognized and based on a full or partial guarantee or letter of credit (depending on the extent of protection conferred) with the risk weight being reduced to that of the counterparty. Where an uncertain payment structure is utilized, or where a mark to market regime is difficult to implement, an additional charge will be levied to cover the payment uncertainty.

US position on credit derivative regulations

The Federal Reserve's Division of Banking Supervision & Regulation, in its letter SR 97-18 (GEN) of 13 June 1997, began by dividing the risk into counterparty credit risk and then into the general market risk arising from changes in the reference asset's value due to factors other than broad market movements, including changes in the reference asset's credit risk.

It defined three position types into which the book (banking or trading book) should be classified:

- open positions
- matched positions
- offsetting positions.

> **Matched positions** are defined as long and short positions in the same credit derivative structures over the same maturities referencing the same assets.

Definition

They are matched only if both legs are either total rate of return products or credit default products. Matching treatment also requires that the default definitions include the same credit events, and that materiality thresholds and other relevant contract terms in the matched positions are much alike.

For the purpose of the Federal Reserve's letter, cash instruments are considered total return products. Hence, a long position in a bond and a short total rate of return swap of the same maturity linked to that bond is a matched position.

If the maturities do not match, or if the swap is a credit default swap, the position is offsetting (as long as the reference asset has the same obligor and level of seniority as the bond).

Definition

> **Offsetting positions** consist of long and short credit derivative positions in reference assets of the same obligor with the same level of seniority in bankruptcy.

Offsetting positions include positions that would otherwise be matched except that the long and short credit derivative positions have different maturities or one leg is a total return product and the other is purely a default product (i.e. credit default swap).

Definition

> Positions that do not qualify as matched or offsetting are **open positions.**

The Fed's view is that the reference asset and the underlying asset are different – the underlying will still be taken as protected as long as both the underlying asset and the reference asset are obligations of the same legal entity and have the same level of seniority in bankruptcy. Banks must show that:

- there is a high degree of correlation between two instruments;
- the reference instrument is a reasonable and sufficient proxy for the underlying asset; and
- the reference asset and underlying asset are subject to mutual cross-default provisions.

Table 7.1 identifies which of the three risk elements is present for each of the three defined position types.

Table 7.1 Credit derivatives market risk framework

	Counterparty credit risk	General market risk	Specific risk
Open position	Y	Y	Y
Matched position	Y	N	N
Offsetting position	Y	Y (some)	Y (some)

Y – risk is present; capital charge is indicated

N – risk is not present; no capital charge is indicated

In summary, all credit derivative positions create exposure to counter-parties and, thus, have counterparty risk. (An exception involves written options where the seller receives the premium in full at the start. Here, risk-based capital is not required, since there is no counterparty risk to the bank selling the option.) For matched positions, counter-party risk is the only risk. The matched nature of the position cuts out the general market and specific risk of the reference asset. Both open and offsetting positions have all three risk elements, but general market and specific risk are much less in offsetting positions than in open positions.

In summary, all credit derivative positions create exposure to counterparties and, thus, have counterparty risk.

Hence, matched positions will not be liable for specific risk charges. For offsetting positions, standard specific risk charges are to be applied only against the largest leg of the offsetting credit derivative and cash positions. That is, standard specific risk charges are not to be applied to each leg separately. (This differs from the Bank of England's approach and, until April, the approach of the Commission Bancaire.) Open positions attract the same standard specific risk charges that a cash position in the reference asset would incur.

Bank of England view on credit derivative regulations

The initial view of the Bank of England was that credit default products must be included within the banking book (November 1996 discussion paper: Developing a Supervisory Approach to Credit Derivatives p. 21). The Bank of England also took the view that in total rate of return swaps, the EU capital adequacy directive did not permit the hedging of one credit risk with a slightly different credit risk. It commented that 'this rather harsh result for "close hedges" is hard-coded in the EU

Capital Adequacy Directive itself, and is also reflected in the Basle market risk amendment standard method.' However, the later adoption in September 1997 of the Basle specific risk modelling amendment appears to have resulted in a modification of this view.

In June 1997 the Bank of England published the initial results of its consultation on the interim capital treatment of credit derivatives. The Bank announced that it would now allow most types of credit default products to be eligible for trading book treatment, as ISDA had requested in its February 1997 comment paper to the Bank. The Bank also said that it felt unable to provide scope for offsets in the trading book, due to the constraints of EU law, but now appears to have revised this view in the light of the specific risk modelling decision discussed below. Following the Commission Bancaire decision, to allow partial offsets where the maturities of the two legs do not match, it seems likely that the Bank may also revisit this area. It has also established a practitioner group with the Securities and Futures Authority (SFA) to address matters relating to the capital treatment of credit derivatives and credit risk generally.

SFA approach to credit derivative regulation

In April 1997, the Securities and Futures Authority (SFA) issued its Board Notice 414 'Guidance on Credit Derivatives'. The notice stated that the variety of products covered by the term 'credit derivatives' made it hard for the SFA to write explicit rules covering all cases and that it had provided guidance to firms on an ad hoc basis, and intended for the time being to continue to do so. Thus, the Board Notice was intended to 'give a flavour of the capital treatments by way of brief explanations and examples'. The primary thrust of the notice was to emphasize the internal control issues which arose from credit derivatives. It makes the point that, traditionally, securities houses have rarely become involved in 'work out' situations and if they become the ultimate owner of the credit risk of a counterparty, they will need to consider if they have the necessary skills in insolvency to make the best recovery possible. The paper also addresses the issue of back-testing actual trading results with expected outcomes. It points out that firms that are familiar with the idea of checking their assumptions about the direction of markets, have been slow to apply similar techniques to credit spreads, ratings migration and default. The paper states that it believes most credit derivative transactions will be trading book items.

The paper goes on to say that "*where a firm has a position in a credit default product that incurs only a specific risk charge, together with a position in the reference asset, the SFA may permit the two specific risk charges to be offset, provided that the credit events specified in the default product are to all intents and purposes the same as those specified for the reference asset.*"

Suppose, for example, the firm has bought a credit default option which pays off if XYZ 8 per cent 1999 bonds default. Suppose it holds the same face amount of the underlying bonds. Then no specific risk charge will be applied, though there will, of course, be a charge to reflect the interest risk of holding a bond (general market risk charge).

Criticisms of the regulatory approach to credit derivatives

A severe criticism which has been made of some regimes such as those in the UK and Germany, for example, is that banks may find that hedging credit risk actually increases their capital requirements. Suppose a credit derivative in the trading book based on a particular reference asset hedges a slightly different underlying asset. Under current rules, this hedge is not recognized. The specific risk from the credit derivative cannot be offset against banking book credit risk from a loan, or trading book specific risk from the slightly different bonds. This actually provides a disincentive to hedge positions.

> **Using credit derivatives to hedge a position may create an extra capital charge.**

Key point

A bank is therefore being punished for hedging its credit exposure. This approach is currently adopted by the Bank of England and, until recently, the Commission Bancaire in France, whereas in the US the Federal Reserve normally only imposes a capital charge on the largest of the two positions.

In addition to this restriction on offsets where the instruments are different, they are also restricted if there is a maturity mismatch, even when the instruments are identical. A ten year bond hedged by a nine year credit default option with exactly the same bond as reference asset is allowed no benefit of offset. Clearly, the protection is by no means complete; yet equally clearly, it is non-zero. In contrast, for non-credit risk elements of the capital rules such as interest rate risk, partial offsets are permitted even when there is only a partial maturity match. Presumably the Commission Bancaire's lead will be followed on this at some stage.

Proposed changes to the regulatory framework by the International Swaps and Derivatives Association (ISDA)

The International Swaps and Derivatives Association (ISDA) has argued (Credit Derivatives: Issues for Discussion in interim Prudential Treatment, 6 October 1997) that, for sophisticated institutions that have developed credit risk models, an internal models based approach to the recognition of offsets is the most appropriate way forward. Even this, however, will still have its limitations given that it will be adopted within a framework that distinguishes between banking and trading books.

ISDA also argues that it would be desirable to develop standardized rules for offsets. First, because any action by the Basle committee on internal risk modelling is unlikely to resolve the problem of the split between banking and trading books. Second, standardized offsets would help institutions which have not yet developed internal credit models. They argue that the most straightforward approach would be to adopt a 'straight line' or 'sliding scale' method for maturity mismatches. Thus, offsets would be allowed to the extent that the maturity of the hedge covers the underlying. For example, a ten year bond hedged by a nine year credit default option would be treated as a 90 per cent offset. Clearly, this approach does not address the question of whether the residual exposure is at the 'front end' or at the 'back end', and ideally the regime should address these issues.

However, ISDA argues in favour of simplicity and conservatism at this stage, as the price for developing fairly quickly a regime which could be put in place to eliminate some of the worst problems currently existing. ISDA also argues in favour of standardized rules for instrument mismatches. Where bonds are issued by the same issuer but of differing seniority, they propose that a simple rule of thumb be employed to permit full offsets in any case where the short position is of more junior, or equal, ranking than the underlying long position. This is because, if the issuer defaults, the holder of the underlying bond will receive a better recovery rate on the senior debt (for example 10 per cent of $100 million principal). They will receive a credit event payment amount of the full principal amount which is reduced only by the smaller recovery level on the more junior form of debt (for example $100 million reduced by a 5 per cent recovery amount of $5 million). This ensures full protection (in this case $5 million recovery on the underlying and $95 million payout on the hedge).

This approach resembles that adopted by the US banking agencies in the rules for recognition of credit derivatives as banking book guarantees. ISDA argues that where the underlying is a loan and the credit derivative hedge is referenced to the same loan, then there is a clear case for permitting full offset. The default events and payout levels will be identical. ISDA proposes that the banking book rules should be adapted to provide a derivatives capital adequacy approach (rather than that for guarantees).

> *ISDA proposes that the banking book rules should be adapted to provide a derivatives capital adequacy approach.*

Thus, in this case, the short credit risk from the credit derivative would offset the loan credit risk on the loan, leaving only a remaining counterparty risk charge to the provider of the credit derivative.

As regards the case where one side of the trade is a loan (or loan based derivative), while the other is a bond (or bond based derivative), ISDA proposes that the approach outlined earlier should apply. That is, the seniority of the loan (since in most cases loans are deemed equivalent to senior unsecured debt or better, given that they are treated as being on equal footing – 'pari passu' – in recovery).

In the case of credit risk arising from counterparty credit risk exposure, but hedged by a credit derivative, ISDA argues that the seniority approach should also apply. Since swap claims are typically treated as pari passu with senior unsecured debt in insolvency, there should be scope to offset underlying counterparty exposures arising from swaps books with credit derivatives which are referenced to assets that are of equal or lower seniority.

Weaknesses of the Basle Accord

It is clear that the growth of credit derivatives, and growth of modelling techniques to measure credit risk, pose a threat to the existing 8 per cent Basle committee ratio. As more 'scientific' measurement techniques develop, the ratio is starting to appear increasingly arbitrary.

> **Key point**
>
> **Beyond the specific question of how to treat credit derivatives is the question of what the arrival of these instruments means for the traditional credit risk framework.**

ISDA has produced a paper (Credit Risk and Regulatory Capital, March

1998) on the Basle committee approach to credit risk. It focuses on a number of weaknesses in the existing regime:

- limited and arbitrary differentiation of credit risk (risk weightings of 0, 20, 50 and 100 per cent);
- the fixed 8 per cent ratio, which is a static and arbitrary measure of the risk;
- no distinction between a one day and a ten year loan;
- limited recognition and safeguards for collateral use;
- a simplistic method of calculating future counterparty exposure;
- failure to allow for the effects of diversification: capital charges are the same for a single $100 million and for a hundred $1 million loans.

The approach recommended by ISDA is to introduce a three-tier framework. The existing structure would be kept, but firms would be allowed to use simplified credit models (to reflect the fact that not all banks have fully sophisticated credit risk management capabilities), or full portfolio credit risk models. They argue that this approach caters for the gradual extension of portfolio modelling by the most sophisticated banks, while allowing for incremental improvements, short of full modelling, in the capital regimes of other banks.

Key point

> ISDA recognizes that, in the case of credit risk modelling, data requirements are more demanding than the market risk models, and the availability of data is much less.

Accordingly, ISDA conducted an informal survey of credit data availability (Elderfield, M. (April 1998) 'Ripe for Reform', *Risk*).

As a result of this survey, ISDA admitted that 'information is much less available for mid-market names and is generally weaker outside the US'.

In fact, this is rather an optimistic statement, since default data is available only on bond issuers. ISDA also points out the difficulty of model validation in the credit risk context – it concludes that a statistically meaningful analysis of one year default probabilities would involve an impractical number of years.

A recent report from the Institute of International Finance's Working Group on Capital Adequacy agrees with the ISDA view that the 1988 Basle Capital Accord is no longer consistent with modern risk management practices. The report argues that bringing the regulatory framework into line with current practices will encourage all banks to strengthen and modernize their risk management systems.

> **Key point**
>
> The aim should be to align economic and regulatory capital more closely than is possible at the moment.

However, the IIF emphasizes that their proposals are for an evolutionary process, not for overnight change.

The main recommendations of the report are:

- the 100 per cent risk weight for private sector credits should be abandoned. Risk weighting of private sector credits should reflect actual credit quality;
- the Basle Accord should be amended over time to permit banks to use their internal credit risk models to calculate the necessary level of regulatory capital, provided those internal models live up to certain standards. The report sets out ten general requirements that the internal credit risk model must fulfil to be deemed satisfactory.

In reply to these various criticisms, the regulators might argue that there are a number of advantages to the present Basle committee approach. Firstly, the approach has the great merit of being simple. This makes it widely applicable, indeed applicable on a global basis. Any more sophisticated approach would inevitably be limited to the major operators. Secondly, and perhaps more importantly, the fact that the 8 per cent is probably excessive in quite a number of cases means that it provides a cushion for other risks which are not separately measured or identified. In particular, the Basle ratios make no allowance for operations risk or legal risk.

Therefore, any move to replace the existing 8 per cent regime by some more sophisticated measurement approach would in turn require the separate imposition of a new capital charge. This would need to cover operations risk, legal risk, and general uncertainty about the bank's management to protect it against all possible dangers.

In this context a paper by David Jones and John Mingo of the Board of Governors of the Federal Reserve System in March 1998 (Industry Practices in Credit Risk Modelling and Internal Capital Allocations: Implications for a Models-based Regulatory Capital Standard) notes the following.

> **Key point**
>
> Those who argue that the 8 per cent ratio is excessive might need to rethink their complaints: a separate capital charge for operations and legal risk might be a high price to pay for more 'accurate' credit capital charges.

Part of the regulators' problem, therefore, is that responding to the growth of credit derivatives means initiating a rethink of the entire 8 per cent Basle regime. This brings the attendant difficulty that any step forward which, in isolation, appears reasonable in the context of the credit derivatives discussion also needs to make coherent sense in the framework of the wider discussion. Otherwise, there is the danger of a series of ad hoc responses which simply complicate the longer-term reform of the agreement.

Banking book versus trading book

One of the trickiest regulatory issues raised by credit derivatives is the boundary between the banking book and the trading book. Up to now, the fact that the trading book had a lot more flexibility than the banking book was not particularly critical. But in the specific area of credit risk, the trading book is much more generous than the banking book. There is thus a very strong incentive to move assets into the trading book to claim more favourable treatment.

One of the trickiest regulatory issues raised by credit derivatives is the boundary between the banking book and the trading book.

One regulator commented that numerous banks were trying to argue that any given set of loans was tradeable, but felt that the liquidity of the market was extremely questionable. This regulator recognized the argument that 'it never will be tradeable unless you allow it in the trading book' but felt that the mark to market process was by no means well established.

Clearly, abuses will need to be prevented, and this can probably be done without undue difficulty by requiring a satisfactory audit trail documenting the original intention to trade the underlying asset, together with evidence of some attempt actually to trade it. But there is a further long-term implication. The greater the proportion of banking assets which are handled out of the trading book – and if the credit derivatives market really begins to grow, presumably this proportion must rise – the greater the pressure to reconsider the whole practice of treating bank loans as instruments that need to be marked to market.

This, in turn, has fundamental implications for the banking industry. Marking the whole loan book to market would be a very considerable upheaval. It would also cause immense problems unless the liability side of the banking balance sheet – i.e deposits – was also marked to market.

It is, therefore, important to assess the impact of shifting the banking book, as well as the trading book, to a model-based approach. Large banks have substantially reduced their capital requirements by securitization without materially reducing their overall credit risk exposures. Also the Market Risk Amendment to the Basle Accord has created additional capital arbitrage opportunities where banks are able to shift assets from the banking book to the trading account and apply their own internal value-at-risk models for capital adequacy calculations on these credit risks.

My view is, from a supervisory viewpoint, the relevant issue is not how easily a sound bank could sell or hedge a single credit instrument of high quality; it is the extent to which a bank under stress could unload the credit risk of a large portfolio of weakened credits. Whereas the markets for secondary loan trading and credit derivatives appear to be expanding and are becoming more liquid, they have not yet been tested by any large bank under severe stress.

Another point to consider is the varying degrees of sophistication employed by banks to assess the loss rate, given default, particularly for complex financial instruments supporting securitization activities.

For example, it is not uncommon for banks to believe that, in the event of default, the [loss] for a subordinate loan functioning as a credit enhancement for publicly issued asset-backed securities would be comparable to the [loss rate] of a corporate loan secured by some other assets (e.g. trade receivables or consumer credit). In the event of default, however, a $25 million subordinate loan supporting a $1 billion pool of securitized assets will tend to exhibit a much greater expected loss rate and loss rate volatility than would a typical $25 million senior corporate loan secured by similar assets. This is because the former will generally absorb a disproportionate share, in some cases (by design) essentially all, of the credit losses on the underlying pool. Given the growing importance of securitization, the risk exposures of some banks arising from credit enhancements may loom large in determining their overall capital adequacy.

Possible regulatory or other problems with credit derivatives

Clearly, there are possible risks and dangers arising from the development of the credit derivatives market. Some of these have much in common with traditional banking problems, and to that extent, present no specific new problems; they are listed below for the sake of completeness. Others arise from the fact that, for the first time, it is possible to create credit exposure to an entity without that entity borrowing or indeed even knowing that credit exposure has been created. This is the genuine new aspect of credit derivatives and one which may raise a number of issues at the policy level.

Problems in 'workouts'

We begin by noting that the use of credit derivatives may, in some cases, complicate the process of 'working out' a default situation. This is not a new problem, in that it has had to be addressed already, in a slightly different guise, namely the trading of distressed loans or debt in the secondary market.

Key point

> Clearly, credit derivative trading can provide a useful exit route for lenders unwilling to participate in what could be a painful restructuring.

This leaves those with a genuine desire to add value to agree the terms of a restructuring. On the other hand, it could delay the process of achieving agreement on the terms of a workout, or even undermine it. A situation could be envisaged where a bank which has credit protection might choose to 'play hardball' to maximize its recovery, secure in the knowledge that if it does tip the borrower into bankruptcy it is covered by its credit protection. One possibility might be a bank which has covenants in a loan which normally it might consider waiving. It might decide not to waive them, in order to trigger a default and collect on its protection. Another possibility might arise if there were a 'basis risk play'. A bank which has credit protection linked to a reference bond might collect under the reference bond payout and then have incentive to play hardball in the loan negotiations, because they have already recovered their losses and the loan recovery would be pure profit.

The timing of trades could have an unsettling effect on restructuring discussions.

There are other tricky issues. For example: What happens if you are in the middle of a restructuring negotiation, and your credit default swap expires tomorrow? Do you trigger a default to safeguard your own position?

The counter-argument is that 'you could only get away with doing that once'. On the other hand, bank managements under pressure have been known to focus purely on the short term rather than think about the long-term consequences of their action.

The timing of trades could have an unsettling effect on restructuring discussions. While it might be helpful in the early stages of a workout, credit derivative trading might bring new banks in when discussions are well advanced. This could be disruptive since newcomers would need time to bring themselves up to speed on the situation and may want to go over ground already covered in earlier discussions. This is often not a realistic proposition. For example, in the UK the lack of statutory protection against creditor demands has tended to introduce a pressure to conclude a workout as quickly as possible.

In the past it has been suggested that trading in the debt of a company which was the subject of a workout should be prohibited; the Bank of England in the London market has resisted this but the same issue might arise in respect of credit derivatives traded on such debt. It might be that the solution is for some form of convention to be drawn up for use when trading the debt of a company which is the subject of a London Approach workout. This might include, for example, keeping the lead bank informed of all trades during a workout.

Further negative aspects of credit trading

Other cases could arise where trading in credit derivatives might cause problems. Three possible situations where problems could arise are:

- carpet-bombing a credit
- crowding-out a credit
- creating/manipulating a credit price.

Carpet-bombing a credit

The first of the potentially negative aspects of credit trading we are going to look at is carpet-bombing a credit.

> **Carpet-bombing** a credit refers to a deliberate attack on the credit rating or quality of a company. Several possible situations might lead to this, among them a hard-fought takeover battle, or alternatively a deliberate attempt to weaken a competitor firm.

Definition

Apples Corporation banks with XYZ Bank. Apples currently does not borrow, and so XYZ has large unused credit lines marked for them. Its major competitor is Oranges Corporation. Both firms are interested in buying Bananas Corporation. Oranges's first act is to approach XYZ's capital markets group and indicate that, for various normal commercial reasons, it wishes to buy a ▶

Example

▶ large credit risk put on Apples Corporation, say, $500 million equivalent. This is allocated against Apples's credit lines and the bankers are delighted – at last some income from the unused credit lines for Apples, even if indirectly. Champagne all round. Next Oranges launches its bid for Bananas. Apples approaches XYZ for finance to put together a counter-bid. It discovers to its horror that XYZ is unable to agree the loan in the time available because the proposed loan exposure, combined with the credit derivative, puts Apples over its existing limit. While it might be possible for XYZ to buy credit protection on Apples in the market, it might not be possible within the very tight timescale required in a bid situation.

For an example, which I stress is entirely imaginary, of how the technique could be used to attack a competitor let us consider a hypothetical software company. Call it, for the sake of argument, Megasoft.

Example

Megasoft has a successful small competitor in a specialized market niche, say widget design. Megasoft would like to buy the firm, but it is not for sale. However, the firm is struggling to finance the next generation of its software. A possible strategy would be for Megasoft to approach the firm's bankers and suggest that, for various commercial reasons, Megasoft requires credit protection against the smaller firm. Megasoft might then recruit one or two key employees of the smaller firm, sufficient to slow its development and force it to seek further finance. If Megasoft have bought sufficient credit default protection to make the smaller firm's bankers reluctant to lend more, the firm might be unable to obtain finance. It would have to file for bankruptcy. At this point Megasoft would be able to acquire the technology very cheaply.

Crowding-out a credit

A further potentially negative aspect of credit trading is crowding-out a credit.

Definition

Crowding-out a credit arises from the fact that parties may be trading in a company's credit without its knowledge.

Even in the absence of any deliberate attempt to fill up bankers' credit lines to a company, active trading in credit derivatives on a corporation might result in its having difficulty in raising finance when it wishes to do so. This could arise if all banks which are familiar with its credit had already sold credit protection on the company. If now the company requires a substantial new credit, perhaps to finance diversification into another line of business or to invest in some new production technique, it might find bankers reluctant to take on further exposure.

> **Thus the credit derivative tail has ended up wagging the dog: a genuine financing requirement has been obstructed by credit derivatives activity.**

Key point

Some traders are enthusiastic about certain possibilities: *"The next good business will be renting a line from someone else who can't use it well."*

On hearing the proposition that the corporate might be concerned to hear about this, the response was robust: *"Nonsense, every time we buy GMAC bonds we don't have to tell them but it has a big impact on our availability lines to them. Why should this be any different?"*

I do recognize that these examples are purely hypothetical. Many uses of credit derivatives will be entirely positive and I do not wish to focus purely on the negative. But I must point out that from past experience in the derivatives markets, credit derivatives often create the potential for abuse and unforeseen problems as well as for improved risk management.

Creating/manipulating a credit price

The third issue is the creation/manipulation of a credit price. The problem here is slightly different: the market for banking credit is not regulated at all. Of course banks are regulated but, unlike the stock market, nobody takes responsibility for trading transparency in the market for credit. Thus the price at which the company commands credit is only visible if it comes to the public syndicated credit market. Once the transaction is done, the only means of tracking the price is through occasional reports in the trade press. For large multinationals the pricing presents little difficulty, but below, say, the top 250 companies in most countries, the picture becomes distinctly murky. There is thus considerable room for manipulation and also room for accidents to happen. In this market, it is easy to imagine cases where the wrong signals about the price of a credit could be sent, accidentally or deliberately.

Key point

> Careful attention by banks to conflicts of interest and the old-style approach to 'relationship banking' may prevent problems emerging. But in an era of transaction style banking some firms may be unduly aggressive. Credit derivatives undoubtedly offer many benefits. But, as with OTC equity derivatives, the structural linkages between the derivatives and the underlying may require careful analysis and, in some cases, preventive action rather than allow inadvertent change to existing financial structures or deliberate market manipulation.

Securities laws

Securities laws are relevant in two main ways to credit derivatives. Firstly, an offer or sale of a security may be involved. This can happen either through the credit derivative itself, in some cases through the physical delivery of a bond, note or participation interest in a loan in settlement of a credit derivative. Therefore, the compliance procedures used in selling a security may be needed. Similarly, the part which is selling the credit risk needs to follow its usual compliance procedures regarding any material non-public information known to it.

Secondly, if after entering into a credit derivative transaction, one of the parties obtains any material non-public information, disclosure to the counterparty may break the relevant securities laws. Clearly, the management priority must be to make sure that securities law compliance procedures are adapted to take into account credit derivatives transactions, where appropriate.

A US banker commented that: "*If ever there's a question of physical delivery of the underlying security, the major US investment banks tend to book the trades out of London. They don't want their unregulated subsidiaries falling into the SEC's net.*"

Pricing of Credit Derivatives

Introduction

It is helpful to begin this chapter with a brief introduction to the different approaches used by market participants to price credit derivatives. There are basically four approaches used to pricing credit derivatives:

- default models based on ratings;
- default models based on credit spreads;
- by reference to guarantee product markets;
- replication/cost of funds analysis.

Each approach has its own strengths and weaknesses, which we will examine, which sometimes result in substantially different pricing across models. The chapter concludes by looking at theoretical pricing models for credit derivatives in some more depth, in particular the replication analysis method.

An introduction to ratings-based default models

These models approximate the probability of the default or downgrade given underlying instruments based on its credit rating and on published transition matrices (for an example of these transition matrices, see Standard & Poor's Ratings Performance 1996: Stability and Transition). To supplement the default or downgrade data, one also needs to make assumptions regarding the impact such an event has on the price of the underlying (i.e. the recovery rate) – this is true whether or not the payout on the trigger event is fixed or variable. Even if the payout is fixed, an expectation of the conditional decline in value is necessary for the dealer to determine the appropriate hedge ratio. One widely used source of default loss data is the Altman dataset.

One widely used source of default loss data is the Altman dataset.

Some of these models use fixed recovery rates, others stochastic (roughly speaking, random) ones. An example of the first approach is Jarrow, Lando and Turnbull (1994), which models the default process based on credit ratings. Specifically, the model assumes that the credit rating of a risky bond follows a Markov chain, and employs a matrix of probabilities for the transition between credit ratings (include default). Das and Tufano (1996) built on this approach with a model that allows for stochastic recovery rate in the event of default. An advantage of this type of model is that it is relatively light in terms of data requirements. Pricing is based on aggregate statistics. Moreover, this approach is a good solution to the problem of inadequate (or missing) issuer-specific data. But this strength is also a key weakness as issuer-level information is lost. So, to the extent that a particular issuer is more or less likely to default than other issuers in its rating category, the model may be unreliable.

An introduction to credit spread based default models

These models use the term structure of an issuer's credit spread over default free instruments of similar maturity to estimate the probability of default or the recovery rate in default. Once this term structure is built, the user can make an assumption about the probability of default over time, to back out the expected recovery rate or vice versa.

Example

If a US corporate issuer's credit spread over the Treasury rate is 1%, the unexpected default losses are 1%, annually or $1 million per $100 million at risk. Hence, for the $100 million risk, if the expected recovery rate is assumed to be 50%, the resulting default probability is 2% annually (2% of $100 million times the default rate of 50%).

One strength of this approach is that once issuer-specific information is available, it is easy to use. Moreover, if one is willing to interpolate based on only a few data points or to make an assumption with respect to recovery rates (possibly based on the Altman dataset), one can back out a time varying default probability based on credit spreads. Arbitrages and anomalies in the term structure of an issuer's credit spread become readily apparent.

A weakness of this approach is that complete term structure is not available for most issuers, so the modeller is again left to interpolate based on only a few data points or to make assumptions based on aggregate data. Another weakness is that the model implicitly assumes the entire spread over treasuries to be due to credit risk. Other factors, such as tax, liquidity and investor appetites, can also have a profound effect on this spread. Determining which portion of the spread is attributable to each factor is not an easy task.

An introduction to pricing based on guarantee product markets

This approach simply looks to other forms of credit enhancement as a reference for the amount by which a guarantor should be compensated, or how much the beneficiary of credit protection should be willing to pay for the commitment of a specific guarantor. The basic idea is that Bank A is willing to pay Bank B 50bps annually to guarantee the debt of XYZ Corporation – a default swap which in essence provides similar protection should be priced similarly.

The strength of this approach is that it is easy to use. The weaknesses are that it is only available for a limited number of names and product structures (specifically, products which offer full default protection only). And even if the credit derivative is a full default swap, there are often material contractual differences which might make pricing by reference to a guarantee contract unreliable.

An introduction to the replication/cost of funds pricing method

This approach prices a credit derivative in terms of hedging costs. The dealer determines the positions necessary to hedge the derivative contract, and how much it costs the dealer to enter into each position. The net hedging cost (plus reserves and dealer's profit and loss) is the price of the credit derivative.

> Assume a dealer pays fixed in order to receive default losses, if any, on a five year note issued by XYZ Corp. Assume the bond yield to maturity of the note is 7%, and the dealer can fund this position at 6.5%. As a first approximation, the dealer would be willing to pay 0.5% for default protection (less a reduction to allow for reserves and profit and loss).

Example

The strength of this approach is that, if a hedge can be constructed, it is the most straightforward pricing methodology available, and its result is the most useful to a dealer. Dealers often employ a hedging/replication approach as one methodology for pricing derivatives. The problem with this approach is that, for many structures, a complete hedge is not available, or would be prohibitively costly. In these cases, a dealer is forced either to rely on a more theoretical approach or to accept the risk that the theoretical pieces will not behave as the whole, or forego the transaction.

Potential variation between the models

To illustrate the potential variation across these models, we can perform a theoretical (mid-market) pricing of a simple credit derivative product under two of the approaches using market data from 11 June 1997.

Example

The product being analyzed is a credit default swap on the 7.25% 1 November 2002 note issued by IBM. Under our hypothetical contract, A makes fixed payments to B based on a fixed rate $10 million notional amount. These payments are made semi-annually and cover the period 1 November 1997 and 1 November 2002: the first payment therefore falls on 1 May 1998. In exchange, B agrees to make payment to A, should there be a default event on the IBM note between 1 November 1997 and 1 November 2002. The payment amount is to be calculated one month after the event of default, and is computed as the difference between: (a) the price at which the note would be trading if its yield to maturity were equal to that of the US Treasury bond note maturing closest to 1 November 2002; and (b) the actual market price of the IBM note. The IBM note is rated A1 by Moody's and A by Standard & Poor's.

Using the term structure of a credit spread approach, the fixed amount paid by A to B is approximately 32bps annually. This is based on the spread to Treasury of the 1 November 2002 note of 33bps and the spread of another IBM note, maturing 1 November 1997, of 42bps. Using the replication/cost of funds approach, A is only willing to pay 3bps annually if it funds at Libor flat. This is based on the forward-start yield-to-maturity of the 1 November 2002 note of 8.85% (compared to 6.78% spot), and the five year forward-start swap rate of 6.82% (compared to 6.735% spot). If A can fund at Libor–10bps, then it is willing to pay 13bps per annum. This illustrates the sensitivity of credit derivative pricing across the modeling approach used, as well as within the same modeling approach.

Theoretical pricing models of credit risk and default swap pricing

Now let's look at some of these credit derivative pricing methods in a little more detail.

Key point

> The market has more experience with the pricing of defaulted risk than casual observation would imply.

All credit sensitive assets embed default put options. In a bond or a loan, the issuer or borrower is the protection buyer and the investor is the protection seller. Compared to a bond or loan, defaulted swaps are distinguished by three properties:

- only credit risk is transferred; default swaps do not have an interest rate component;
- principal is not invested; default swaps are leveraged and self-funding;
- default swap payments are subject to the default risk of the swap counterparty.

Just like a bond or a loan, investors must be able to assess whether a spread premium is fair compensation for credit risk. While the credit spread is effectively the markets of the fair price of credit risk, there are also an increasing number of quantitive models that can be used to arrive at appropriate fair values of this risk.

The first generation models of credit risk rely on default and recovery information.

Default-based models

Early models aimed at quantifying credit risk are based on the work of Fons (1994).

The Fons formula   Fig 8.1

$$P = \sum_{t=1}^{N} \frac{S_t C + S_{t-1} d_t \mu (C+F)}{(1+i)^t} + \frac{S_N F}{(1+i)^N} \text{, where}$$

S_t = the probability of striving to year t without defaulting (one minus the *cumulative default rate* for year t; $1-D_t$)

d_t = the probability a bond defaults in year t given it has survived to year t without defaulting

i = the yield on a Treasury bond with N years to maturity

C = the coupon on a bond with N years to maturity

F = the face value of the bond

μ = the recovery value of the bond in the event of default

Spread = $(C - i)$ = the risk neutral spread, or expected loss, for a par bond

Credit rating agencies collect exhaustive historical data on both defaults and recoveries. Recovery rates are computed with historic data on defaulted bond prices and broken down by industry sector and seniority. In comparison, default rates are broken down by credit rating.

The Fons model (see Figure 8.1) is simply a variation of the standard bond pricing formula, except each cash flow is weighted by its expected value. The expected value of a 'risky' cash flow is based on the likelihood (the default rate) and severity (the recovery value) of loss. Credit rating agencies collect exhaustive historical data on both default and recoveries. Recovery rates are computed with historic data on defaulted bond prices and broken down by industry sector and seniority. In comparison, default rates are broken down by credit rating. A key assumption of the Fons model is that the credit sensitive asset is held to maturity. If default occurs, the bond is sold at a price equal to its recovery value.

Risk neutral investors only require a spread wide enough to cover the expected loss.

The appeal of the Fons-type models is that they can be used to quantify the expected loss of a risky bond. This is computed by setting the bond's price to par and solving for the coupon C. The expected loss is the coupon less the yield of a default free treasury of comparable maturity $(C - I)$. The expected loss is also the risk neutral spread since a risk neutral investor would be indifferent between the default free asset and the risky asset, for the investor is fully compensated for the expected loss.

The market commands spread premiums in excess of the expected loss. This is because investors are not risk neutral; they require additional compensation in the form of excess return and liquidity premium. Furthermore, investors need to be compensated for the uncertainty surrounding point estimates of default probabilities and recovery values. In Figure 8.2 we have separated the components of bond spreads

Fig 8.2

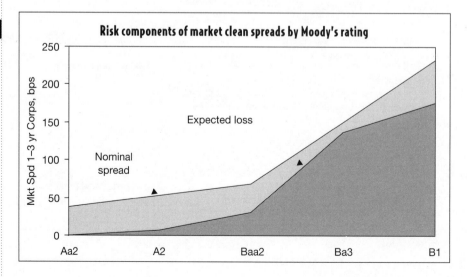

Risk components of market clean spreads by Moody's rating

between excess returns and liquidity, and default risk. Lastly, note that this model can be used to assess the default risk probabilities implied by the market price of traded instruments.

Expected loss modelling can be put into an option context. For example, when an investor buys an investment grade bond, he is implicitly writing a deep out-of the-money default put option. Unfortunately, an option approach is more analytically appealing than it is practical, for two reasons. First, traditional approaches such as Black-Scholes should not be expected to work well. The assumption that default risk is lognormally distributed is not supportable. Expected loss distributions stemming from credit risk are infamous for their 'fat tails'. Second, an option model does not value the residual portion – excess spread liquidity premium – of the bond's spread.

> **Traditional expected loss modelling does not account for mark to market risk.**

The limitation of expected loss modelling is that it assumes the bond is held to maturity or default. It also fails to capture any variability of the bond's credit rating over its life, which can be significant for longer term assets. Moreover, since default risk is very low for investment grade assets, the model is predicated on an event that is not only highly unlikely but also has a limited contribution to the asset's actual price variability. In sum, the model is not consistent with mark to market concepts such as Value-at-Risk (VaR).

Rating transition models

Rating transitions capture the variability in credit rating changes over time.

Rating transition models are credit models that are mark to market in spirit. In recognition that default risk may not be the immediate source of credit risk, rating transition models quantify the effect of expected rating changes on bond returns. Rating transitions measure the probability that a credit's rating will migrate to a new rating over a given period of time. For example, a single-A rated bond has a 93.4 per cent probability of retaining its rating for the next year and a 4.72 per cent probability of becoming triple-B in one year.

The transition data can be used to compute expected returns over a specific time period. This return is the sum of the bond's probability weighted price changes, where the price changes are the current spread less the spread associated with a given rating times the duration of the bond. Figure 8.3 shows the expected returns formula.

Fig 8.3

Expected returns formula

$$\text{Expected return} = \sum_{i=1}^{N} P_i[(S-S)D], \text{ where}$$

i = rating category (e.g. Aaa, ..., Ba3) P_i = probability of rating i at horizon
S_i = spread of bond with rating i   D = modified duration of bond at horizon
S = initial bond spread

Example

Consider a single-A bond trading at a spread of 60bps. Its one year expected return is 57bps, which represents a 3bps loss. The reason for the loss is that the rating migration is skewed to lower ratings: the credit has a greater probability of experiencing a downgrade than an upgrade in its rating (see Table 8.1). This results in a loss of principal as the bond has an expected spread of 60bps. Had the credit curve been steeper (flatter) between single-A and triple-B bonds, the expected return would have been lower (higher).

Table 8.1 One year rating transition probability for A-rated credits

Current rating	Aaa	Aa	A	Baa	Ba	B	Caa–C	D
A	0.03%	1.3%	**93.34%**	4.72%	0.51%	0.05%	0.03%	0.03%
Market spread (4yr)	40	45	**60**	75	100	250	n.a	n.a

Key point

Rating migration data are imperfect measures of a given credit's rating volatility.

Like default and recovery data, rating transition data are derived from historical experience. They provide a consistent method of following trends in credit quality. While the transition data are highly detailed, covering several years and rating classifications, their level of aggregation may still be too high. For example, within a rating group, a specific industry sector may not be well represented by the market, e.g. in the single-A sector, commercial banks have been trending to double-A in the wave of strategically-orientated mergers. This trend is not captured in the migration data.

Stochastic models

Stochastic credit models attempt to reconcile the limitations of static models. The appeal of these models is that they are arbitrage free and rely on established methods of asset pricing. Most rely on a Markov process, which is consistent with the notion of first order market efficiency. However, they often rely on two many parameters to implement efficiently. For example, a default-based model may be adjusted for the variances in default probability associated with rating transition migrations. Moreover, these models may require rather arbitrary volatility inputs. Consequently, these models will not yield consistent results across end user because the data inputs and assumptions are not the same. Currently, the models may be well suited for risk management but not necessarily for pricing individual bonds or defaulted swaps. Over time, we expect stochastic models to become increasingly important, particularly as credit risk transfer extends beyond the liquid markets.

The replication pricing approach

Default swap pricing does not require an analytical model. Default swap pricing is more straightforward than suggested by analytical models. While these models provide objective and systematic methods of analyzing credit risk they also have several shortcomings. In particular, the parameters (default probability, rating migrations, recovery values) are not contemporaneous. Rating changes seldom occur without advance notice from the agencies; spreads partly adjust to these watch listings. Several other factors – technical conditions, event risk, overall market conditions, liquidity premiums – that determine a bond's spread are not captured by these models.

> **Market credit spreads capture default and recovery properties.**   **Key point**

Default swap pricing is based on arbitrage relationships between actual market instruments. As such, market credit spreads drive the pricing of default swaps. Cash market pricing of credit risk is consistent with theoretical pricing models:

- the term structure or shape of most credit curves reflects the change in cumulative default rates over time;
- differentials in industry sector spreads can be partly explained by differentials in recovery value.

The term structure of credit spreads should reflect the change in default risk over the life of the asset. Figure 8.4 shows the relationship between cumulative default rates and the triple-B yield curve. The positive slope of the credit curve is consistent with the rise in default risk; the marginal default rate increases each year. For speculative credits, marginal default rates tend to decline over time, a fact that explains why credit curves in those markets are frequently inverted.

Fig 8.4

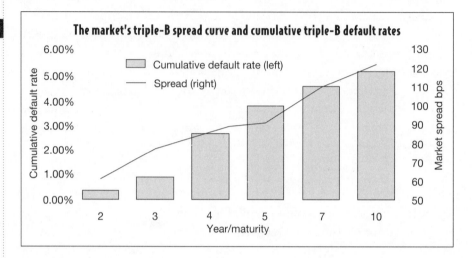

The market's triple-B spread curve and cumulative triple-B default rates

Market pricing also accounts for recovery value. The easiest way to test this is to examine the spreads of bonds with the same credit rating, but different recoveries. Figure 8.5 shows market spreads for sectors with different recovery values and the same probability of default. Specifically, we have grouped low-triple-B rated bonds in the seven to ten year part of the index by industry sector and compare the average bullet spread for each sector to the average recovery value for the sector. As the figure shows, spreads are inversely correlated with recovery values. This relationship is not only statistically significant, but somewhat surprising given the imperfect aggregation of the Standard Industry Code (SIC) groupings (i.e. phones are grouped in Communications along with media, and all REITs are grouped in Finance).

Relative value

Rather than use complicated models to estimate default probability we can use a simple method. A credit default swap is rather like the financed purchase of a bond since there is no cash outlay and there is no regular stream of coupons to compensate the investor for holding his cash and assuming some sort of credit exposure.

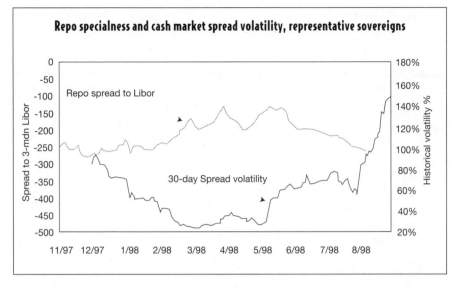

Repo specialness and cash market spread volatility, representative sovereigns

Fig 8.5

All things being equal, the swap should trade at the same level as an asset swap on the same bond. Take a liquid corporate credit that trades at a spread of 65bps, over US treasuries. Assume that the asset swap rate is 35bps – now the corporate bond can be swapped to a floating rate of Libor +30bps.

A bank which is hedging as a principal or intermediary an illiquid credit position on the same bond might offer to pay a credit spread of 40 over Libor for default protection via a credit default swap. The bank offers to do so if the cost of the next best alternative to reducing exposure or the assumed cost of not hedging at all is more than 10bps.

Since the credit swap pays the investor an extra 10bps, for assuming a similar credit risk to the bond, you might say that it is better value. Dealers compare a credit default swap's relative value against an asset swap rather than against a bond's underlying spread over treasuries since the credit swap is an unfunded transaction requiring no initial cash outlay.

This is an important point. If the investor was to try an unfunded position in the bond, they would have to access financing through the repo market. Since it is possible to finance corporate assets at Libor flat, the investor's net spread income is the spread against Libor rather than the spread to treasuries.

The benchmark against which credit default swaps should be judged is the asset swap. The difficulty is to convince clients that 10bps is enough compensation for the much greater illiquidity risk in a credit default swap. For investors who like to buy and hold, illiquidity is not much of a concern. But investors with shorter time horizons may demand an illiquidity premium. For investment grade names and a seven year term, the premium would probably be around 10bps a year.

The liquidity premium is an important factor in the pricing process. Credit derivative traders are more like cash traders than other option traders. They determine the theoretical price of the structure and then step back and assess the liquidity of the underlying hedge. If there's no liquidity, there's no hedge and if there's no hedge, the spread widens right out.

The liquidity premium is an important factor in the pricing process.

There are situations where it has taken two weeks to place any type of hedge against the credit default swap. The credit default swap market is linked to the asset swap market in terms of relative value. However, there are other factors which an asset swap does not depend upon:

- probability of default
- recovery value
- credit quality of swap counterparty (not so important)
- correlation (between protection seller and reference asset issuer).

The asset swap approach to pricing

Arbitrage relationships underpin the pricing of default swaps because market participants can replicate default swap exposure using cash instruments. This greatly simplifies pricing; we do not have to price the default option explicitly, as the expected value of credit risk is already captured by the cash market credit spread.

Default swap pricing is not model dependent because we assume the underlying cash market is efficient, on average. Asset swap levels provide a pricing source for pricing default risk.

These levels provide a context for relative value, because reference assets have transparent prices. This approach also makes it possible to tie expectations about cash bond pricing to expectations about the pricing of a default swap – an important consideration when constructing hedges. Figure 8.6 shows how a default swap exposure can be replicated.

Key points

- Sell default protection (sell default swap) = Buy risky bond, sell risk free bond.
- Buy default protection (buy default swap) = Sell risky bond, buy risk free bond.

In Figure 8.6, the investor is selling default protection. In a replication trade, the investor:

- purchases a cash bond with a spread T+Sc for par;
- pays fixed on a swap (T+Ss) with the maturity of the cash bond and receives Libor;
- finances the position in the repo market. The repo rate is quoted at a spread to Libor (L–x);
- pledges bond as collateral and is charged a haircut by the repo counterparty.

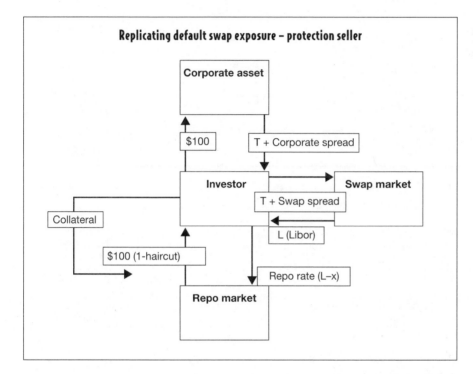

Replicating default swap exposure – protection seller

Fig 8.6

Each of the four trade components may not be self-explanatory to investors unfamiliar with hedging and financing. Below we expand upon those steps.

Interest rate hedge

The interest rate swap component of the trader eliminates the duration and convexity exposure of the cash. If we did not hedge this exposure, the trade would simply equate to a leveraged long position in the fixed rate corporate (T+Sc–(L–x)).

> Swap hedges are more efficient interest rate hedges than treasury hedges.

Key point

There are three reasons why the interest rate hedge is accomplished through a swap and not a treasury:

■ *Libor is a consistent benchmark of value* – there are anomalies associated with pricing an asset to a treasury given the high volatility of its term financing. As a result, Libor-based benchmarking is increasingly becoming standard. Libor is also the benchmark for the bank loan market.

■ *Lock-in cash flows for term of swap* – if the short were structured with treasuries and repo, the financing would need to be rolled every three months.

■ *Favourable economics* – it is cheaper to hedge with a swap than a treasury. The cost of the hedge is net cash flow, not the cash market spread between the asset being hedged and the spread on the swap to the treasury. It may seem strange to pay the swap coupon (T+Sc) rather than the Treasury coupon (T). But note, the swap hedger will receive the lower treasury repo rate. Table 8.2 compares hedging strategies. 'Current carry' is the net saving from hedging with a swap rather than the treasury on a three month term basis.

Key point

Investors need to consider Libor repo differentials when hedging interest rate risk.

Table 8.2 Swap versus treasury interest rate hedge – current carry of swap

Mat	Three month repo	Three month Libor	Swap spread	Current carry	Mat	Three month Repo	Three month Libor	Swap spread	Current carry
5-yr	4.80	5.69	55	34	10-yr	4.60	5.69	62	47
Old 5-yr	4.80	5.69	51	38	10-yr	4.65	5.69	55	48

Current carry is (Libor–Repo) – Swap spread. Pricing on 14 August 1998

Financing of cash position

Since we are replicating a swap, we have to introduce financing into the trade. This is accomplished with a corporate or sovereign bond repo. The purchase of the bond is funded through a collateralized loan to a repo dealer. There are two important components to this trade:

■ *Haircut* – the lender charges a haircut – the difference between the securities purchased and money borrowed – for the loan. Haircuts vary widely according to the type of collateral, the credit of the counterparty, the term of the repo agreement, and the type of funding. It is designed to protect the lender from market risk of the collateral. The interest earned on the haircut is compensation for assuming the counterparty risk. Moreover, since the haircut represents the capital in the trade, institutions with the cheapest cost of capital will be able to assume the credit exposure for the lowest net cost.

■ *Repo rate* – the financing charge is the repo rate for the specific collateral. The rate will vary depending on the demand to borrow (or lend) the security. We have denoted this rate as L–x, since several liquid credits have repo rates that are usually, but not always, less than Libor.

Table 8.3 Cash flows of default swap replication

	Receive	Pay
Cash bond	T+Sc	$100
Swap hedge	L	T+Ss
Repo transaction	$100	(L–x)
	Sc–Ss+x	

Sc = Corporate spread; Ss = Swap spread. Assuming no haircut.

Close examination of Table 8.3 reveals that the cash flow nets to (assuming a haircut of 0 per cent for simplicity):

$$(Sc - Sc) + x$$

If the repo rate for the bond was Libor flat ($x = 0$), the exposure would simply be the asset's swap spread (Sc – Ss).

As we alluded, several 'on-the-run' credits can finance through Libor. Thus, for the same reason that a treasury may trade 'special' in the repo market, certain corporate and sovereign bonds will trade below general corporate or sovereign collateral, as they are the assets of choice for hedgers.

> The remaining cash flow looks very much like the payment made to a protection seller on a default swap, a simple annuity stream expressed in basis points for the life of the trade.

Key point

If the bond defaulted, the repo would be terminated and the investor would lose the difference between the purchase price and recovery price of the bond. The asset swap pricing approach is an efficient way to gauge default swap fair value because if actual default swap pricing differs too much from synthetic pricing, arbitrage opportunities will emerge. Profits from mispricing can be arbitraged most efficiently by market makers – who are subject to the lowest transaction costs – and institutions with the highest credit quality, which can exploit the relative advantage in funding costs.

Table 8.4 Cash flows of default swap spread lock

	Receive	Pay
Cash bond (Short)	L–20	L+45
Default swap	85	
Net	20	

The mispricing between the markets has to be large enough to account for both basis risk and transaction costs. This pricing approach provides a means to assess value in the default swap market. Table 8.4 shows how an arbitrage might exist: The table uses the example of a five year cash bond trading at L+45. Five year default protection for the bond is quoted at 85/90bps. Thus a protection seller would pay an implied repo rate of L–40, and the spread lock would equate to 20bps of arbitrage profit. This trade assumes a term corporate bond repo market, which may be difficult to find in most markets. The repo would most likely have to be rolled on a short-term basis, rather than for the term of the swap. For this reason, asset swap pricing is a discrete-time model rather than a continuous-time model.

If this arbitrage did exist, the protection sellers would eventually drive the default swap premium down toward the asset swap level, eliminating the mispricing between the two markets. Aside from arbitrage constraints, default swap spreads will vary with supply and demand conditions, just like other types of financial instruments. Generally, hedgers will pay a funding premium to lock in the cost of a term hedge.

Implied repo premiums for credit default swaps

I have intentionally denoted the financing rate as L–x to emphasize that implied term financing rates are an important component of default swaps. Both bond spreads and swap spreads are given in the market. Likewise, the default swap quote is given, leaving the term financing rate for the underlying reference credit as the unknown variable.

The spread, x, can be thought of as the implied term financing spread relative to Libor or the implied repo premium in the default swap. The more a default swap is trading over the asset swap level, the higher the repo premium.

This spread is meaningful for both relative value considerations and gauging market sentiment. If the repo premium is high, it can indicate higher levels of distress or exposure in a particular credit, as the market is willing to effectively borrow it at expensive levels. Moreover, since a swap is leveraged and constrained by arbitrage profits, its pricing will usually adjust more quickly than cash market pricing.

> *Implied repo rates can reveal information about market exposures in a credit.*

Implied repo rates can reveal information about market exposures in a credit.

Table 8.5 Implied repo premiums for writing default protection for five years

Credit	Rating	Spd	Asset swap	Prot (bid) 31 August	8 July	Impled 31 August	Repo 8 July
Ford	A1/A	T+96	L+18	27	22	9	6
GMAC	A3/A	T+98	L+21	26	22	5	7
Philip Morris	A2/A	T+115	L+38	51	50	13	8
News Corp	Baa3/BBB–	T+145	L+68	80	50	12	12
Tele Comm	Baa3/BBB–	T+96	L+19	55	30	36	10
Time Warner	Baa3/BBB–	T+115	L+36	70	40	32	10
RJR Nabisco	Baa3/BBB–	T+300	L+223	275	n.a	52	n.a
Rep. of China	A3/BBB+	T+365	L+288	420	n.a	55	n.a
Rep. of Korea	Ba2/BB+	T+955	L+878	800	n.a	78	n.a

Table 8.5 presents the implied repo premiums for a diverse group of five year credit default swaps. Note that over the brief period from 8 July 1998 to 31 August 1998, credit markets were under unusual stress. Fixed rate spreads gapped dramatically with the collective event risk of Russia, Japan/Asia, and Latin America. As the table illustrates, the implied repo premium to Libor increased for most of these credits.

For example, Time Warner (TWX) default protection widened out by 30bps to 70bps. This change in premium was not fully reflected in the change in the asset swap level; at L–32, the repo premium rose from L–10 on 8 July. Investors willing to write protection on the credit would lock in better term financing than in July. Conversely, investors seeking to buy protection in the name would have to pay more to short the credit. Default swap premiums can also be viewed as forward asset swap spreads, assuming Libor flat is the market's funding benchmark. For instance, TWX's premium of 70bps can be thought of as a forward spread, which compares to the 31 August par spread of 38bps. Thus, the default swap market is pricing in almost a doubling of TWX's asset swap spreads.

Key point | Default swap premiums can also be thought of as term forward spreads.

The cost of capital and the proxy for the risk free rate

Investors may want to integrate their cost of capital into the valuation of a default swap. Compared to credit sensitive cash assets, it may seem as though default swaps introduce a second risk because Libor, not the risk free treasury rate, is the benchmark for pricing. But default swaps entail financing, and Libor is the market's benchmark for the short-term cost of capital of the marginal borrower.

The notion of the risk free rate is often academic. For example, in S&P index futures arbitrage models, the 'risk free rate' is Libor, not the three month Treasury bill rate. One way to view a default swap is a long position in a 'risky' floating rate bond, which trades at Libor plus a spread and a short position in a 'riskless' bond, which trades at Libor flat. This bond is a good proxy for the risk free rate because its coupons will continually reset to the funding rate benchmark-Libor.

Key point | From a cost of capital perspective, relative borrowing costs are important. Investors can compare the collateral market versus on balance sheet financing when valuing default swaps.

A protection seller's exposure in a credit could simply be replicated with a floating rate loan to a specific creditor, which is funded at the short-term borrowing rate of the institution making the loan. In this analysis, collateral and repo market considerations are unnecessary. The return for credit risk is the net spread, after deducting the creditor's cost of funding the asset on its balance sheet.

The financing market for credit sensitive instruments

Since implied financing is an important vehicle in default swap valuation, the intricacies of credit sensitive financing markets are a considerable component of default swaps and their relative value.

Key point | An understanding of the dynamics of specials markets is critical to accepting the important role of default swaps.

A sector's specials market is a less liquid and more volatile reflection of its cash market. The inherent limitations of credit sensitive markets financing illustrate how important default swaps are in completing these markets. The ability to hedge risk with another vehicle should complement both the existing and new market. A review of these markets reveals that liquidity in the default swap market compares very favourably to that of the financing market.

Financing market conventions

Financing trades can be implemented in a variety of ways: standard repo agreements, buy/sell backs, bonds borrowed, tri-party repo. We generally refer to all as repos.

> A **repo** is a repurchase agreement whereby an asset (the collateral) is simultaneously agreed to be sold and repurchased at a future date for a stated rate of interest or price.

Definition

Figure 8.7 illustrates the basic structure of a repo. In a repo, collateral is traded for cash. The collateral 'seller' borrows cash and lends collateral (a repo). The collateral 'buyer' borrows the collateral and lends cash (a reverse repo). The repo bid/offer refers to the rate at which the collateral can be bought. Hence, the bid is higher than the offer, since it is the cost of borrowing (or buying) cash and selling collateral.

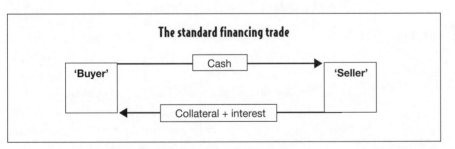

The standard financing trade

Fig 8.7

The financing market has its own language. The collateral backing may be nonspecific (general collateral or G/C) or specific (special). The G/C and specials markets are related since G/C provides a reference rate for a sector (see Table 8.6). G/C rates are related to other short-term money market rates, whereas specials rates are determined by the supply and demand for a specific security (collateral).

A bond is 'expensive to borrow' when buyers receive very low rates of interest on the cash they lend in exchange for the collateral they borrow. Specials rates fall when there is high demand to borrow (or short) specific collateral. For this reason, it is often expensive to short bonds: the repo special rate received on the cash lent is well below the coupon (or yield) paid on the bond that is borrowed.

Table 8.6 Overnight general collateral rates, spread to Fed funds

Trsy/Mtge	Bid/Offer	Corporates	Bid/Offer	Emerging market	Bid/Offer
US Treasury	+5/–10	AA–A	+20/+5	Sovereign	+65/+25
Gov. agency & GNMA	+16/–6	BBB	+35/+15	Corporate	+60/+25
Mortgage (deliverable)	+20/–0	High yield	+50/+25		
Fed funds is the Federal funds rate opening quote on 7 October 1998					

The corporate credit sectors

The majority of traditional corporate bond investors do not participate in the repo market. There is a general rule about the specials market for corporate bonds: the largest issues have the greatest potential to be shorted, and subsequently trade special. This tendency argues that even cash investors should prefer holding the larger issues of a given credit since they could get spread performance from repo squeezes. When the credit is under severe stress, however, all of the outstanding issues have the potential to trade expensive in the repo market.

Corporate general collateral

The key participants in the corporate G/C market are dealers and money market investors.

This is an overnight market, though term does trade occasionally. The bid/ask spread for overnight corporate collateral is around 10bps. Corporate bond dealers finance the bulk of their inventories, at general collateral rates, in the repo market. Collaterized borrowing is a cheaper source of funding than a loan from the parent. The counterparties for these financings are money market funds and other types of short-term investors who invest in corporate repo for its relative spread over treasury and mortgage repo. Dealers also manage matched books and frequently hold a basket of longs, anticipating that at least one bond in the basket will become special.

The key participants in the corporate G/C market are dealers and money market investors.

Corporate specials

The corporate specials market is by appointment. When a counterparty wants to borrow a specific security dealers must 'work an order', checking for availability with customers' portfolios (usually securities lenders) to assess the availability of the collateral. It is common to find that quotes vary widely by dealers. This process exists because it can be treacherous to short small issues. The average issue size of bonds in the investment grade bond index is only $230 million. Consider that one $20 million short requires that almost 10 per cent of the issue be found and held by an investor who will lend the securities. It is not hard to see that the specials market is frequently one-sided, dictated by the offered side.

> When a counterparty is looking for specific collateral, the bid/ask spread can widen, with the bid anchored near G/C. Liquidity spreads can be as wide as 70bps in the overnight market.

Key point

As a result of the relatively small sizes of most issues, the corporate specials market is characterized by low liquidity, with securities lenders providing the bulk of the liquidity to this market.

The market is viable, albeit imperfect. Several names trade actively on an overnight basis. Among the most actively traded names are Ford, GMAC, Merrill Lynch Associates, Chase, Household Finance, and IBM. These names are benchmarks for their sectors. Ford and GMAC are the largest issues in the investment grade market. Global issues also trade more actively, for they are larger. New issues trade actively as dealers may short oversubscribed deals and hedge funds 'flip' new issues. Three month term offer for nonspecific Ford and GMAC is currently 5.25 per cent, while specific collateral is offered at around 5.00 per cent.

Investors can benefit from being strategic in this market. For example, a good time to lock up term financing of a long position is immediately following the underwriting of a 'hot' new issue – a time when there is a fresh supply of shorts.

Note that when financing a long, the worst case on funding costs is to pay the G/C rate. Currently three month term is trading at around Libor flat for single-A credits. As a rule, longs trading at G/C should be funded on an overnight basis, providing the investor the flexibility to immediately earn better carry if the issue begins to trade special. If necessary, 'stub risk' can be hedged with Eurodollar futures. Conversely, when shorting a security, it's better to lock in term borrowing, if the security is not trading overly special.

Haircuts

For a repo agreement the New York Stock Exchange requires that a 20 per cent haircut be posted for corporate securities. Investors can lower haircut charges by entering 'bonds borrowed' trades. The economics of these trades are identical to repos, but they are not subject to NYSE rules. 'Good faith' haircuts are determined by the counterparties' corporate credit departments and range from 2 per cent to 50 per cent, with well capitalized borrowing posting 5 per cent margins for investment grade credits.

Emerging market and sovereign sectors

Sovereign financing markets are more active and have more participants than their corporate counterparts. They are used for hedging, leverage, and relative value trading by a range of market participants.

The issues are larger – most global and Eurodollar bonds are at least $500 million, while several Brady bonds issued are several billions. Sovereign credits are also more risky, as measured by both their higher spread volatility and lower ratings.

A large community of investors borrows and lends bonds. Market neutral investors will use the repo market to arbitrage both intersector and intrasector yield curves as well as spreads between Brady bond issues and Eurodollar bonds of the same credit. Since sovereign credit spreads can be as volatile as the underlying interest rate benchmark, dealers are more likely to hedge their inventory. Not only are sovereigns easier to borrow than corporates, but it is easier to rationalize hedging spread risk. Term markets are also active, particularly in the 'big three' – Mexico, Brazil and Argentina.

Table 8.7 shows current sovereign bonds trading 'very special' or at least L–200. Collateral haircuts are approximately 15 per cent in most of these markets. The bid/ask spreads in most of these markets range from 25 to 50bps. The Russia Euros, a credit under severe stress, are trading at 0.25/00 markets. These bonds are very expensive to short, but for a long position the 0.00 per cent asked rate looks inconsequential relative to the total yields, as well as to the coupon payment uncertainty of the issues.

Since most spread-type hedges suffer from low or negative carry, expectations about spread volatility underpin decisions to hedge.

Key point

> The repo spread premium in the financing market is highly correlated with cash market spread volatility.

The 30 day spread volatility can be the historic spread volatility of 14 representative emerging market bonds. Bonds in the index include: VEN 27, BRAZ 27, ARGEN 27, RUSSIA 07, ARGEN 03, MEX 26, MEX 07, BRAZIL 08, ARGE 06, MEX 08, MEX 01, RUSSIA 01, ARGEN 99 and PAN 27.

The spread repo spread to Libor is the average number of basis points the bonds are trading below Libor in the overnight market (the repo premium). Interestingly, 75 per cent of the variation in the repo premium can be explained by the volatility in the cash market spread, based on regression analysis. Thus, cash market spread volatility is a very important determinant of repo specialness.

Table 8.7 Sovereign bonds trading 'very special'

Bonds	Rating	Issuer size	Market	Strpd sprd	O/N Repo bid	O/N Repo ask	Spd to O/N Fed funds
Argentina, Rep 03	Ba3/BB	$2,050	Global	632	2.75	2.25	325
Argentina, Rep 06	Ba3/BB	$1,000	Global	878	2.25	2.00	3350
Argentina, Rep 27	Ba3/BB	$2,750	Global	782	2.62	2.38	312
Brazil, Rep 01	B1/BB-	$750	Global	1058	0.88	0.62	488
Mexico BNCE 04	Ba2/BB	$1,000	Global	744	2.25	1.75	375
Mexico UMS 08	Ba2/BB	$1,500	Global	692	1.00	0.50	500
Mexico UMS 04	Ba2/BB	$1,000	Global	577	1.75	1.25	425
Mexico UMS 26	Ba2/BB	$1,750	Global	756	2.75	2.50	300
Russia Euro 01	B3/CCC	$1,000	Euro	4799	0.25	0.00	550
Russia Euro 07	B3/CCC	$2,400	Euro	3229	0.25	0.00	550
S Korea, Rep 03	Ba1/BB1	$1,000	Global	657	0.25	0.00	550
S Korea, Rep 08	Ba1/BB2	$3,000	Global	779	3.50	3.25	225

21 August 1998, Spread to Fed funds is spread through Federal funds target.

Hedging credit default swaps

The following key issues need to be considered when hedging credit derivatives:

- *Illiquidity* – it may be tough to get the instruments in the open market. The underlying bonds may be illiquid. After a credit instrument is purchased, it is tough to get out of it at a reasonable price.
- *Bid/Offer spreads* – may be high since the underlying instruments are not liquid.
- *Gapping behaviour* – credit spreads are not continuously traded. A 'credit event' causes the spread to gap considerably over a short period of time. This is a reflection of the 'matrix pricing' technique often used in fixed income.

- *Shorting bonds* – to hedge, one needs to short bonds. This may or may not be possible or cheap.
- *Volatility* – volatility of credit spreads is much higher than that of the corresponding yields.

Although the pricing of credit derivatives represents complexities, it is unlikely that these will limit the development of the market. Hedging, however, is a different matter. To date, the difficulty in hedging has limited the size and cost effectiveness of many types of products. By way of looking at the workings of the market, it may be helpful to look at a specific example.

Example

This example looks at the 7.95% K Mart bond maturing 1 February 2023 and the 7.125% US Treasury bond maturing 15 February 2023. Consider a situation where an investor expects K Mart's credit quality will improve over the next year. He enters into a credit spread swap with a dealer.

  The dealer will enter into a series of deals to hedge the exposure created by the swap. The initial hedges are shown in Figure 8.8 below.

Fig 8.8

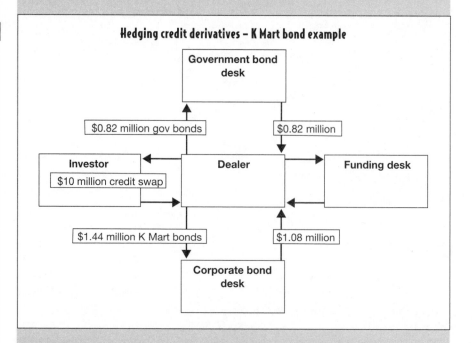

Hedging credit derivatives – K Mart bond example

As can be seen from Figure 8.8, the trades needed are as follows:

- Borrow the Treasury bonds, in order to short sell the Treasury bonds.
- Borrow additional funds, and use the proceeds to purchase the underlying K Mart notes.

The size of the K Mart note trade and the Treasury bond trade depends upon their respective durations. In this example, the face amount of K Mart bonds bought is around $1.44 million, for a cash price of $1.08 million. The face amount of Treasury bonds shorted is $0.82 million. Hence the need to borrow $0.26 million to make up the cash shortfall.

A few comments on the above example

Figure 8.8 shows the initial hedging only. The hedge must be dynamically managed. Because of convexity (i.e. the non linear relationship between prices and yields), the hedge is adjusted as the yields of the underlying instruments change.

The above deals do not leave the dealer perfectly hedged. In particular, during the time the dealer holds K Mart bonds, it receives the coupon payments on them (7.95 per cent per annum). But if the K Mart bonds default, the dealer loses these coupon flows. This is typically solved by the dealer charging the investor a premium for that risk.

The existence of the credit derivative does not change the fact that in order for the investor to take a view on K Mart's credit, the underlying bonds must be bought. The key difference is that the dealer, rather than the investor, does the actual purchase. This is why leveraged transactions, as discussed in this chapter, are the only way to get around the fact that the volume of corporate credit derivatives is limited by the size of the underlying market.

9

Practical Credit Default Swap Applications

Introduction

This chapter concentrates on the practical application of default swaps, from an investor's viewpoint. Because default swaps are currently the most common credit derivative instrument trade, they warrant a chapter to themselves. An investor can use credit default swaps to create synthetic assets, such as a synthetic floating rate notes, and they can also be used by investors in the hedging of cash assets, i.e. hedging existing bond portfolios. The chapter concludes with a look at how default swaps can be used to capture arbitrage opportunities between cash, repo and default swaps. An actual case study 'The Case of Korea '03s' is chosen to illustrate arbitrage.

Creating synthetic assets

Investors can use default swaps to create synthetic assets. For unleveraged investors, the generic type of strategy is to write default protection, post the required margin and invest the remaining principal in a near-money-market equivalent asset. Triple-A rated floating rate credit card asset backed securities are usually the cheapest type of asset for creating synthetic assets. These assets have negligible default risk because of early amortization features and credit enhancement achieved through subordination (12–15 per cent) and excess servicing (3–6 per cent).

The combination of a floater and a default swap equate to a synthetic floating rate note.

The potential loss of premium associated with early amortization events is mitigated by the floating rate structure.

The combination of a floater and a default swap equate to a synthetic floating rate note.

Investors are motivated to use default swaps to create synthetic assets for two reasons:

■ *Relative value* – at times, a synthetic asset is cheaper than the cash market equivalent. This is especially true when the implied repo rate in the default swap is trading Libor. As a result, an investor can monetize the repo premium implied in the default swap, without having to finance the trade.

■ *Access deeper market* – default swaps enable investors to tap a market that is larger than that of tradeable securities. A desired credit exposure that is not available in the cash market can be synthetically created.

> Since out-of-favour or volatile credits tend to trade at higher repo premiums, investors can use default swaps to take views relative to the forward credit spreads implied by the default swap market.

Given the historically low levels of interest rates and flatness of the yield curve, a disproportionate share of new issue volume has been both fixed and dated. As a result, the supply of corporate floaters and short-dated fixed rate bonds has been concentrated in a handful of, usually finance, credits. The number of credits available in the default swap market is larger since the exposures that financial institutions need to transfer are broader. For example, banks may want to hedge a revolving line of credit with an industrial credit by buying protection on the underlying credit, rather than sell the loan and risk affecting a banking relationship. Additionally, I anticipate a large per cent of the commercial paper backstop market will be securitized via default swaps – again, providing another source for synthetic assets.

Table 9.1 Using default swaps to create synthetic floaters

Credit	Rating	Term	Protection	AAA-rated ABS FRN	Synthetic floater	Asset swap	Pick up
Anheuser Busch	A1/A	1-yr	8	L+8	L+16	L–1	17
May Dept. Store	A2/A	3-yr	21	L+12	L+32	L+25	9
Key Corp	A1/A–	3-yr	18	L+12	L+30	L+25	5

In Table 9.1, the economics of synthetic floaters are compared to asset swaps. As shown, the synthetics trade much cheaper. For example, the 1-year Anheuser Busch synthetic floater is trading at L+16, or 17bps above its asset swap level.

The investor is subject to spread duration risk of the ABS floater and the change in the premium of the default swap.

For fixed rate synthetic assets, I recommend investing principal proceeds in the AAA-rated asset backeds of 'name brand' servicers or agencies' benchmarks (which fund as well as L–50 in the repo market). Investors can also receive fixed on an interest rate swap or buy Eurodollar futures.

Investors may view selling default protection as carrying more risk than investing in the comparable cash assets due to counterparty risk of the swap. For a protection seller, the risk introduced by a highly-rated counterparty is negligible. If the counterparty defaults, the maximum loss to the seller would be the premium, if any, on the swap. Rating agencies have been asked to rate only a handful of default swaps, mainly because default swaps are off balance sheet. Moody's approach is similar to that used for credit linked notes. The agency uses an expected loss approach to rate a swap. For a swap, the expected loss is the sum of the expected loss on the reference credit plus the expected loss on the swap.

> **The expected loss on the swap is the product of the probability of default and the mark to market on the swap.**

Key point

This figure is very close to zero, since default rates for single-A rated or better counterparties have run at less than 0.10 per cent for the past several years. Hence the rating of the reference credit is most likely the credit rating of the default swap.

Hedging cash bond exposure

One of the most important applications of default swaps is hedging. As noted earlier, credit risk can be very difficult to hedge, in part because of its heterogeneous nature.

> **All hedges incur basis risk; the basis risk in a default swap stems from the volatility in the implied repo premium.**

Key point

Since this premium will be more volatile for low-rated and distressed credits, these types of credits will be subject to more basis risk than their investment grade counterparts. As a rule, the cheapest time to implement a hedge is when the market is not concerned about the risk.

Constructing a hedge versus an index

One way to illustrate the effectiveness of default swaps in hedging is to assess how a hedge performed (see the example below).

Consider a hypothetical hedge employed by a money manager benchmarked to the Merrill Lynch Corporate Aggregate (C0A0), who held 10% of the portfolio in Hilton Hotels (Baa1/BBB). In September 1997, this $500 million portfolio held $50 million in Hilton five year bonds, which were originally purchased at a discount and now have a four point gain. The remaining 90% of the portfolio matches the index in terms of duration and credit quality.

Note that the hedge in the above example can be viewed generically. For instance, one way to reduce a portfolio's exposure to the REIT market would be to buy default protection on the most representative credit.

The exposure of the portfolio can be brought back to index levels with either an outright sale of the bonds or a hedge using a default swap.

There are three reasons why the portfolio manager might opt to hedge rather than sell:

- to avoid adverse tax events (four points of capital gain position);
- to hedge is inexpensive (basis could work in favour of hedge);
- high transaction cost due to low liquidity in the cash market (credit is out-of-favour).

Table 9.2 shows the components of the hedge – the swap, the cash bond and the benchmark. In September 1997, five year default protection on Hilton cost 55bps. Since the cash bond asset swapped to L+60, the implied repo rate was L+5. Hence, the bond was cheap to short. Over the course of the year, the fixed rate spread widened to T+170bps and the premium on the swap rose to 120bps. The implied repo premium on the swap shifted dramatically – since the implied repo rate changed to L–25, the hedge netted an additional 30bps gain, simply due to the shift in basis.

The index 'spreads' are also shown in Table 9.2. Fixed rated spreads widened 43bps over this period, but since interest rates fell by more than that amount, the portfolio had a modest gain of $1.48 per $100 of exposure.

Table 9.3 compares the unhedged portfolio to a portfolio hedged with a default swap. In the unhedged portfolio, the Hilton exposure represents $50 million or 10 per cent of the total portfolio value. Spreads widen by 47bps in this portfolio compared to 43bps in the index. In the hedged portfolio, $50 million of protection is purchased, thereby leaving the portfolio flat the Hilton exposure.

The loss due to spread duration risk on the cash position is more than fully offset by the change in the premium on the default swap.

Table 9.2 Example of hedge of Hilton exposure versus index

	Def. swap premium	Hilton 7.7 7/02 (T+Spd)	(DV01 3.4) (L+Spd)	Corporate (T+Spd)	Index (DV01 5.9) (L+Spd)
Spreads, bps					
15 September 1997	55	90	60	57	18
28 August 1996	120	170	100	100	25
Spread change	65	80	40	43	7
Price effect, $					
Chg due to Spd duration	$2.21	–$2.72	–$1.36	–$2.55	–$0.42
Chg due to I-rate duration	$0.00	$3.14	$0.00	$4.03	$0.00
Total price change	**$2.21**	**$0.43**	**–$1.36**	**$1.46**	**–50.42**
Hedger is buying protection of Hilton (55bps is offered side quote and 120 is bid side quote).					

As a result, the hedge outperforms the unhedged exposure by almost a quarter of a point ($1.59 – $1.37). Note that the hedged portfolio also outperforms the 100 per cent index matched portfolio ($1.59 versus $1.48). The reason for this is that the index is longer, and consequently suffered more from spread duration risk.

Table 9.3 Hedged and unhedged portfolios – 10% Hilton, 90% 'Market'

	Unhedged (T+Spd)	Portfolio (L+Spd)	Hedged (T+Spd)	Portfolio (L+Spd)
Spreads, bps				
15 September 1997	60	22	58	20
28 August 1996	107	33	101	27
Spread change	47	10	44	7
Price effect, $				
Chg due to Spd duration	–$2.57	–$0.51	–$2.35	–$0.29
Chg due to I-rate duration	$3.94	$0.00	$3.94	$0.00
Total price change	**$1.37**	**–$0.51**	**$1.59**	**–$0.29**

Hedging and tax implications of default swaps

In the earlier example, it is assumed that the bond position being hedged had a four point premium. If the bond was liquidated, the gain would represent a tax event to investors subject to capital gains tax. Since the bond's price experienced a slight appreciation ($0.43), the investor may want to leave the hedge on. Had the bonds been sold in September, the tax event would have equated to $1.40 per $100 ($4* the 35 per cent corporate tax rate). For the $50 million exposure, the tax penalty would equate to a rather startling $700,000 cash outlay (which compares to the $550,000 difference between the unhedged portfolio and the

Default swaps are an important tax management tool.

index). For this reason, it may be prudent to use a default swap to hedge even when it is trading at fairly high repo premium.

Default swaps are an important tax management tool.

Arbitrage – default swaps, cash and repo

As discussed in Chapter 8, credit default swaps can be used to arbitrage mispricing in the cash and financing markets. Several types of arbitrage can be structured on the assumption that the swap market is forward looking.

Key point

> At times, default swaps pricing is sufficiently inefficient to result in profitable arbitrage.

In default swaps, there are two basic 'market neutral' strategies:

- buy protection (short), buy the cash bond (long), and fund with repo;
- sell protection (long), sell the cash bond (short), and borrow the bond at the repo rate.

'Conventional wisdom' is to sell protection when implied repo premiums are high and buy protection when implied repo premiums are low.

Trading the implied repo premium – The Case of Korea '03s

Default swaps tend to widen before cash spreads because the demand to buy protection causes premiums to rise to a level wide enough to attract protection sellers.

Table 9.4 shows the relationship between a default swap, asset swap and repo for five year Republic of Korea (BB1/BB+). The asset spreads are to Libor and are based on comparable maturity swap rates.

In Figure 9.1, the trend in these spreads is shown, since the bond was issued in April 1998. Notice that from April to May the bond's spread was fairly stable, as was its repo rate. However, the credit began to show signs of stress in July – not in the cash market, but in the default swap repo market. The default swap premium traded significantly over the asset swap level. On 21 July, investors could sell premium at levels much

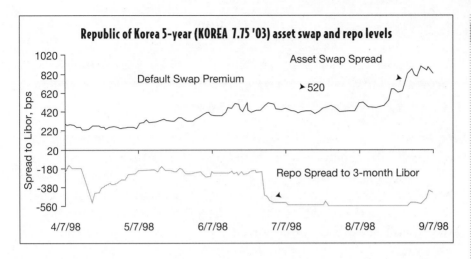

Fig 9.1

wider than cash bonds. Synthetic term financing of long positions could be locked in at L–176bps. The premium of 520bps could also be viewed as the forward asset swap spread. To monetize the difference between this forward spread and spot spread, an investor would sell protection at 520bps, and short the cash bond at 344bps.

The trade has negative carry because the bond is trading at zero in the repo market.

Table 9.4 Components of an arbitrage trade on Korea 8.75 '03s

Date	Default swap	Asset swap	Imp. repo	O/N repo (Ask)	Carry
14 Sept. 1998	800/900	818/810	L+18	1.00	–478
26 Aug. 1998	550/650	600/569	L+50	0.00	–618
7 Aug. 1998	440/540	433/428	L–7	0.00	–581
4 Aug. 1998	490/540	366/359	L–124	0.00	–444
21 July 1996	520/560	344/340	L–176	0.00	–392
8 April 1998	335/410	306/287	L–29	4.25	–114

Notice that the implied repo rate on the swap was trading at L+50bps in late August, suggesting the market no longer needed to aggressively bid up for hedges indicating that spreads were expected to fall negligibly. The trade could be unwound at a profit. The default swap position lost 130bps (520–650) and the short made 225bps (569–344), resulting in a net gain on 95bps.

The total profit is less than 95bps, due to the negative carry of the trade and the fact the DV01 of the cash bond was lower than the DV01 of the swap.

Conclusion

The purpose of this chapter and also this book has been to demystify credit derivatives with an analysis centring on one of the most common credit derivatives – the credit default swap.

Credit risk transfer entails levels of complexity not found in other types of financial risks. The market, however, is very experienced with the pricing and analysis of credit risk: this type of risk has been transferred through the sale of marketable bonds for several years. With a bond, the issuer is the buyer of credit protection and the collateral on the debt is the bondholder's claim to the assets of the firm. With default swaps, only credit risk is transferred and the collateral is the haircut on the swap.

Key point

> **Are credit default swaps to this decade what interest rate counterparts were to the last?**

While the market is too new to answer this question completely, it is clear that default swaps share many parallels with interest rate swaps.

Defaults swaps are important financial instruments because:

- they allow credit market participants to manage credit exposures in new ways;
- they represent a necessary complement to both the cash and financing markets for credit sensitive instruments;
- default swap pricing – as the Republic of Korea example illustrated – can reveal fascinating market information about expected credit risk.

In my opinion, credit default swaps use will increase steadily. We now have an efficient way to take a pure view on credit spreads. With the new ISDA docs, liquidity should improve.

INDEX